"Hey there Moms-I've got good news: Go
Him, to trust Him. And Aimee's book, *The*
you need to get started. Aimee shares her heart througn ...
through how to lean into the rest God has promised. Thank you, Aimee, for this valuable resource!" --Rachael Carman, Author of *How Many Times do I Have to Tell You?*
RachaelCarman.com

"The word 'peace' is used in the Bible over 400 times. We find rest in peace, but it isn't natural to us, hence all the reminders. We need a model to follow and a reminder of who we are in Christ. *The Restful Homeschool Resolution* does just that for those who need a model to remember who they belong to and what they are called to do."

--Robert Bortins, CEO, Classical Conversations

"As we have traveled the country meeting and interviewing parents for *Schoolhouse Rocked*, it has become clear that homeschooling leaves many moms feeling inadequate, weary, and overburdened. Aimee offers practical hope and help for these moms, including myself. Not because she has it all figured out, but because she knows the One to go to amid the angst. Matthew 6:33, "...seek FIRST the kingdom of God and His righteousness..." This is it! This is how we discover true rest in all areas of life. And this is the narrative that Aimee beautifully weaves throughout this book as she takes us on a 21-day journey guiding us through truths that can only be found in the Word of God."

--Yvette Hampton, Producer and Host of *Schoolhouse Rocked: The Homeschool Revolution*

"My hopes for my homeschool are generally not my reality. This book will challenge your expectations of obtaining success in your own efforts while offering a gentle mentor to walk you into a closer relationship with God as your strength and shield. Aimee asks the hard questions but only because she's walked through them herself. This humble offering of God's truth is refreshment for the soul, and what every homeschool mom needs to read every year!" --Betsy Strauss, Blogger at FamilyStyleSchooling.com

"Aimee has put together a simple, practical, and effective tool for the homeschool mom to study and implement the biblical command for us to REST - specifically in the context of our homeschools. In her 21-day study, Aimee has put things into bite-size chunks that are meaningful and achievable – and biblically focused. I can't wait to share this with my mom friends and possibly start a restful group of my own!"

--Mary Prather, HomegrownLearners.com and SQUILT Music Appreciation

"A must-read book for any homeschool mom that longs for rest and peace in her home, her homeschool, and her heart." --Sarah Avila, Blogger at MyJoyFilledLife.com

"*The Restful Homeschool Solution* is a breath of fresh air and a must-read for all homeschooling moms. Aimee's writing is real and honest. This 21-day journey allows busy homeschooling moms to find the rest and rejuvenation we are all desperately seeking - not within worldly pursuits but in the loving, merciful arms of our Savior. Not only will this book give you the wisdom to transform your homeschool, you just might end up transforming your heart and entire life too."

--Heather Bowen, Founder of LifeofaHomeschoolMom.com and Conferences for Moms

"As an author, mother of 4, and homeschool educator, my daily responsibilities can feel overwhelming at times. *The Restful Homeschool Resolution* inspired me to embrace true rest and prioritize worship as part of my daily routine. A must-read for the Christian homeschool mom!" --Kirsten McTernan, Author of *Homeschooling: You CAN Do It!* Mcternan.com

"So many times, rest has beckoned like unreachable treasure. If only we could find the right map, we could find rest. Not only does Aimee show us the true definition of rest, but she gives us a beautiful map that points us toward that true rest. And joyfully, we are able to revisit her map as often as we need to refresh, revive and renew ourselves in that perfect rest." --Deven Vasko, ProfessionalHomeEducator.com

"I love the *real story* feel to this. It's not preachy or pie in the sky stuff. Are you spying on my life and heart?" –Jenifer L., homeschool mom

"I underlined/highlighted most of it. Great stuff!" --Karen S., homeschool mom

"These devotions have been spot-on for this mama's heart." –Gina M. homeschool mom

"God used this book when I was needing a friend to ask me the hard questions. It was like having a conversation with you, and I'm so thankful!" –Amy V., homeschool mom

"This book has been a sweet and gentle call to me to keep my eyes on the Author and Finisher of my faith. It is such a refreshment to my soul!" –Nicole N., homeschool mom

"You offered small, easy steps to incorporate into our days to help us seek God more and become more restful. I feel encouraged and supported, not judged."

-Jill R., homeschool mom

"It's an engaging devotional that is not churchy or cheesy. It has both spiritual and practical applications all in one book!" –Angie W., homeschool mom

THE RESTFUL HOMESCHOOL RESOLUTION

21 Days to Transform Your Homeschool

AIMEE SMITH

THE RESTFUL HOMESCHOOL RESOLUTION

For more information:
https://www.aimeesmith.com

Cover design by Juan Francisco Irusta, 99designs.com
Cover photo by Annie Spratt, unsplash.com
Interior design by Derek Murphy, diybookformats.com

ISBN: 978-0-578-56825-6
First Edition: September 2019

For Mother

You taught my heart to seek Jesus.

Enjoy your perfect rest with Him in our eternal home.

and for Katie Ruth

You've been in my heart for a decade.

Now it's time to bring you home.

CONTENTS

ADDITIONAL RESOURCES

Access additional resources for your 21-day journey with *The Restful Homeschool Resolution* on our private page:

www.aimeesmith.com/21days
Password: **SeekJesusFirst**

Download free printables for reminders to seek Jesus first.
Find an upcoming online book club.
Access links referenced in this book.

ACKNOWLEDGEMENTS

To Aron, without you, this book would not exist. You have kept me going when I wanted to quit: both in writing and in homeschooling. You have rescued me from my many technical mistakes and from my inner critic. Most importantly, you have modeled the love of Jesus in giving up yourself for me.

To Jackson, Malyn, Micah, and Caleb, we did it! Thank you for completing school assignments, finishing your chores, cooking dinner, and refilling my coconut, so many times on your own initiative. Thank you for giving me space alone to write, editing my multiple rough drafts, and rejoicing over every little publishing victory along the way.

To Dad, your *well done* echoes a future greeting from our heavenly Father. Thank you.

To Janet, you are a homeschool pioneer in our local area. I am thankful you and Bryan were faithful so we can stand on your shoulders in educating another generation.

To Leigh, Hailey, Maggie, and Anna, you've walked with me through the struggles that led me to pursue true rest. You've known my many weaknesses since we were little and shown me the true meaning of brotherly (sisterly!) love. Thank you for sharing my excitement of this publishing process.

To Maegan, thank you for convincing me I could actually write a book, coaching me through the process, and encouraging me all along the way.

To Shannon, my editor, your keen eye for detail is a blessing to cover my many mistakes. Thank you for our enjoyable conversations about the nuances of our language.

To Church of the Highlands, Pastor Chris Hodges, and Pastor Blake Lindsey, thank you for teaching me to seek Jesus first through 21 Days of Prayer.

To my review and launch teams, you will see your influence throughout this book. Thank you for your honest feedback and support to share this message of God's rest.

To my prayer team, thank you. May Jesus receive all glory and honor.

preface

I RAN INTO THE HOUSE, ARMS FILLED WITH DAFFODILS. I searched for my mom with the vibrant yellow flowers, freshly picked from down the hill in the woods behind our home. My gift was not an attempt to gain approval. I simply wanted to enjoy her presence and her smile as she placed them in a vase to display in our kitchen.

Years later, I gained understanding of her enjoyment in the moment when my daughter formed a habit of bringing me the most beautiful bouquets of weed flowers. Mothers don't care if the gift is perfect. We simply enjoy our child's enjoyment of seeking our presence.

Throughout the years, daffodils have become a continual source of joy and rest for me. Their unfolding marks rest in the midst of struggle, faithfulness in annual expectation, and a new thing in the changing season. Their burst of yellow in the dreariness of winter is a sign of faith in the midst of despair, joy in the midst of suffering, hope in the midst of trouble. As they faithfully bloom in late January, they promise a new season is coming. Year after year, they give confident expectation that God is always doing a new thing. Collecting daffodils for my kitchen is an annual habit reminding me of the rest and joy God offers to my soul.

In my adult years, a new habit has graced the beginning of my year: 21 Days of Prayer. It's another burst of light in the dreary midst of winter. Building this habit required perseverance. I have felt the sting of inconsistency and failure many times, but I have continued in a relentless pursuit of Jesus.

Seven years into this seasonal habit, in January 2016, this book was born. For the previous year, I had been in a season of forced rest from my homeschool leadership endeavors. With my chronic illness and my mom's battle with cancer, my family needed all of my limited energy.

Homeschooling felt nearly impossible in that season. Sibling squabbles, a struggling learner, and constant chaos abounded in our home. I worked hard to fix the problems. I researched new curriculums, created new chore plans, and formed new parenting tactics. A sense of unrest, however, remained in my heart as I exhausted my efforts to transform my homeschool.

In January 2016, I had also been practicing the skill of

writing to obey God's call to enter this new sphere of ministry and tell my story. I had bought a domain for a website to begin blogging, but it remained empty. The day before 21 Days of Prayer began, I heard the Holy Spirit's whisper to *just begin*.

Every morning, I woke early and spent time in the Bible, worship, and prayer. Then I started writing. I never had a plan. Just a single word or verse from the Holy Spirit. I wrote, quickly edited, published it on my blog, then shared on social media before I could change my insecure mind.

I had no plan, but like the daffodils, bulbs were buried in the soil of my soul. In my dark places of fear, anger, and despair, God had planted bulbs of hope in His Word. I knew His Word must be true even though my circumstances claimed otherwise.

As I reflect on that season three years later, I clearly see the new work God was doing. I now live in His joy and rest that bloomed in the midst of my struggle. It's certainly not a perfect rest. I will enjoy that one day in heaven. Every January and August, I still participate in 21 Days of Prayer. God continues to use the words in this book to draw me closer to Himself and to help me see Him transform my heart and my family. The words I wrote were His Word of hope for my weary soul, and I am delighted to now share them with you.

One year after unknowingly writing this book, I handed my mom her last daffodil. A few days later, she entered her eternal rest with Jesus. God used that burst of color to shine His light on my heart in the dreariest of seasons. That single daffodil reminded me He always offers His rest in the midst of any difficult life circumstance.

In my early days of grief, we transplanted daffodil bulbs from my mom's childhood home to the woods of my new home. We dug them up on my 39th birthday, then they sat in the garage for days. Finally, I resolved it was time to plant them. My daughter was preparing for an academic competition, so we edited and recited as we dug. I smashed my finger, pretty sure it was actually broken, but I pressed on. Juggling responsibilities, caring for my child, and pressing through pain, I fulfilled my resolution. Now, I eagerly anticipate the first glimpse of yellow every winter.

Resolution. That's what this is: a resolution to seek Jesus first for a restful homeschool. The next twenty-one days might be harder than you expect. You might feel a sense of failure at some point along the way. Get back up and keep going. The pursuit will be worth it. You will eventually see the bloom and experience God's rest.

God is not looking for your perfection. He wants you to enjoy being in His presence. In His presence, there is fullness of joy. His presence will go with you into normal daily life, and He will give you rest.

Spring is coming, momma. God is doing something new. Do you see it? He is ready to do a new work in your heart and your home. Draw near to Jesus, and He will draw near to you. Seek Him first, and all these other things will be added to you. You will receive His rest in the midst of your difficult circumstance.

Look for the glimpse of yellow, that faint burst of His light. Seek Jesus first. Watch for Him to transform your heart and your homeschool.

seek Jesus first

our resolution

THIS WILL BE THE YEAR. I lean back in my chair and smile at the neat stacks of books on my pristine desk. My shiny new planner is filled with goals, lists, and routines for the new year. Last year's books are put away, and I reviewed each child's progress while setting their new educational goals. I even took time to hand-write our family vision for education.

This will be the year. Beautiful books fill a basket for our family morning time. I finally found *the* math curriculum for my struggling student. The chore list is revised and visually inviting. Our new schedule for school days will certainly ensure smooth and easy sailing.

This will be the year. My heart feels at least somewhat rested and refreshed. Exercise, sleep, and drinking plenty of water top my priority list. A new devotion book and journal are stacked with my Bible.

This will be the year. Oh yes, our homeschool has been a mess in the past. But as the new year dawns, whether it's the beginning of the school year or the calendar year, my hope is renewed. My resolve is fresh. My dreams seem certain.

This will be the year we follow the plan. This will be the year my heart remains calm. This will be the year we enjoy a truly restful homeschool. This will be the year.

Two months later. . .

If I make it that long. Who am I kidding? It's probably no more than two weeks. Two days perhaps?

All hope of a restful year is lost. My desk is covered in dust and cluttered with stray papers. Coffee stains and ripped pages scar the beautiful planner. Goals, lists, and routines? Ha! We're just trying to survive another day.

Our morning read-alouds appear to simply be opportunity for group squabbling. I remember what I learned last year: finding the right curriculum is not the cure-all solution for math. The house is a mess, and my well-constructed chore plan is already forgotten. Schedule? We'll eventually drag ourselves out of bed and accomplish something so we can check off another school day.

And my weary homeschool momma heart? Oh my, must I be honest and transparent? Let's just say my heart gives evidence, quite loud and clear, that I'm still in need of much sanctification. I can reach the end of the day and realize I even failed at the basics of caring for myself physically, and my neglect of spiritual care might be even greater.

Before 9am, I'm texting my husband saying I really can't do this anymore. I have to give myself a timeout so I won't injure these young people I love more than anyone. I know I'm running on empty. *Restful* homeschool? That's a lofty dream. I'm debating whether I should quit homeschooling altogether.

Sure, those books, websites, and podcasts about restful homeschooling are appealing. They beckon our hearts to view home education as something far more than school at home.

I bought in to the dream. I'm a firm believer in creating an environment for enjoyable family time. My heart's desire is to foster a love of learning in my children. My husband and I view academics as only one component of education, and we endeavor to cultivate an atmosphere that draws our children toward lifelong learning. The dream of rest is good.

I homeschool because I *enjoy being with my children*. My vision is to daily teach them *how to learn* and *how to live* an abundant life with Jesus. Our family motto is to *reflect Jesus.*

On the average day, however, I forget. The messy reality of life makes a restful homeschool seem impossible. Relationships are hard. Parenting is hard. School is hard. The restful homeschool I imagined becomes a fleeting dream.

What is your reaction to the promise of a restful homeschool?

- Impossible! Experience has taught me rest and homeschooling are mutually exclusive.
- I'm trying. When I find the right plan, I think we will be restful.
- If they would only. . . If my children would stop fighting. If my husband would be more involved. If only. . .
- Maybe, just maybe. I think a restful homeschool is possible, but I'm not sure how to get there.
- I want more! I have glimpsed moments of rest, and I crave more of them.
- That's us. We have journeyed through the seasons, and we are learning a restful homeschool is possible in the midst of a messy life.

Since you picked up this book, you must have a longing deep within to cultivate rest in your home. Perhaps you, like me, have tried creating rest for yourself and your family. Your efforts have been good but end up lacking.

You have heard your Savior's gentle whisper, "Come to Me, and I will give you rest," and you believe it must somehow be true. You know God loves you and has good plans in store for your life. You attend church, read your Bible, and pray.

But your heart is still restless. Unrest could be in the form of weariness, anxiety, depression, or anger. Temptations to strive harder or give up completely can lead your heart from the rest Jesus has for you. An over-packed schedule and information-overloaded culture threaten to unravel your soul.

Along the way, you realize the state of your heart affects your entire family. You cringe when you hear, "If momma ain't happy, ain't nobody happy," because you know it's true. Who you are impacts your homeschool more than what you do. Maybe your lack of a restful homeschool is connected to a lack of a restful heart.

In a sense, you begin to grieve over the state of your heart. Despair sets in as you admit your external behaviors are evidence of an internal reality. Stress. Headaches. Anxiety. Yelling. Fatigue. Drill sergeant. Depression.

Oh friend, will you choose to see these cues of unrest as a gift? They are an invitation to believe God can do *far more abundantly beyond all you ask or imagine* (Ephesians 3:20). Your dream of a restful heart is not impossible. When your stress levels rise, it's a cue you're seeking rest in a fruitless place. Your cues of unrest are cues to seek rest in Jesus alone.

What type of rest are you seeking?

When you think about rest, what images fill your mind? My mind is drawn toward a day on the beach with my toes in the sand, a few hours in a hammock with a good book, or a full night of uninterrupted sleep. And a restful homeschool, what does that look like? It could include calm children snuggled on the sofa for a read-aloud, nature sketching in your vegetable garden, or everyone gathered around the table diligently completing math assignments.

Are you settling for rest that is a mere shadow of what Jesus offers? It is possible you're seeking rest in a mere break or orderly circumstances, but true heart rest comes from Jesus alone. Organization, routines, plans, they're all good. Keep pursuing excellence in your work as a homeschool mom. Just don't expect them to do in your heart a work that only Jesus can accomplish.

The rest Jesus offers is a gift wrapped in the fruits of the Holy Spirit. A restful heart is loving, joyful, peaceful, patient, kind, good, faithful, gentle, and self-controlled. As you submit in obedience to Him, your heart becomes more restful. As you learn to trust Him, fear and despair begin to melt away.

The rest Jesus offers is intertwined with work. When He invites us to come to Him to receive rest, He also invites us to wear His yoke. It's a yoke connecting us to Him to accomplish a task as a younger ox would work beside an experienced ox in the task of plowing. His rest is a beautiful irony of peace in the midst of work, joy in the midst of darkness, love in the midst of conflict.

The rest Jesus offers is just the beginning. Learning to walk in His rest is a life-long journey. You experience a glimpse of it and begin to crave more. You walk in rest for a season then give in to the temptation to fret and worry. You slowly learn to recognize your common cues that your heart is not at rest, and you learn to lead yourself back to Jesus.

True rest is a work of the Holy Spirit which occurs out of view. True rest comes in the midst of the busyness of life. True rest begins small and grows through a lifelong journey. Refuse to settle for a shadow of the rest Jesus offers you.

How can you cultivate a restful heart?

Yes, a truly restful heart is the work of the Holy Spirit, but you do have a role to play. Jesus has invited you to receive His rest, but you must accept the invitation.

> *"Come to Me, all who are weary and heavy-burdened, and I will give you rest. Take My yoke upon you, and learn from Me, for I am gentle and humble in heart, and you will find rest for your souls." Matthew 11:28-30*

Cultivating a restful heart begins with having a real relationship with Jesus. As you walk through the coming pages, you might wonder if you really *know* Him or if you merely know *about* Him. If you're not sure, check out my story at www.aimeesmith.com/relationship-with-Jesus to learn how you can begin this life-changing relationship.

That's the first step to receiving the invitation Jesus has given you: Come to Me. Your first step to truly knowing Jesus is just the beginning. Throughout life, you will continually return to Him as you seek rest for your heart. In Jesus' invitation from Matthew 11, I see three principles that are crucial to pursuing rest.

Seek Rest in a Person. *Come to Me.* Where are you seeking rest? If you're seeking rest in calm children, a clean home, or Instagram worthy activities, you're bound to be disappointed. This is the shadowland of rest. Yes, they're restful, but they're only a glimpse. True heart rest only comes from being near to

Jesus Himself. These next twenty-one days will be all about drawing nearer to Jesus.

Receive Rest as a Gift. *I will give you rest.* How are you trying to create rest? Family experiences, an uncluttered home, breathing space in your schedule. They're all good. They're all important. Keep pursuing the things which promote peace for you. Just don't settle with the shadow of what you can create. The rest Jesus offers is far better, and it is a free gift for you.

Cultivate Rest through a Journey. *Take My yoke upon you, and learn from Me.* What if becoming restful requires time? Our instant gratification culture tempts us to want everything right now. But learning from Jesus, the One who is gentle and humble in heart, is a process. Growing in rest is the result of walking with Jesus. It's a journey, and rest grows with time.

Will you make one resolution?

Seek Jesus first. This one choice is the restful homeschool resolution. It might sound like a simplified Sunday school answer, but don't underestimate the power of a single choice. This one resolution could transform your homeschool.

> *"But seek first His kingdom and His righteousness, and all these things will be added to you." Matthew 6:33*

Jesus was responding to people's concerns for necessities of daily life – food, drink, clothing. He never claimed those details weren't important. He encouraged the people to seek God first and trust Him to provide for their needs.

In your life as a homeschool mom, many cares fill your mind. Details for household management, meal preparation, lesson planning, and character formation are all important. You should focus your time and energy on doing your work heartily. You should seek the things which make for peace in your home. Just be sure to seek Jesus first.

There's no one-size-fits-all method for seeking Jesus. He does not require a thirty-minute quiet time, first thing in the morning, with a lit candle and steaming cup of coffee. He wants your heart and your attention.

Seeking Jesus first can be a whispered prayer as you roll out of bed. You could sing along with a worship song as you get dressed for the day. Spending time in God's Word could involve a paper Bible, Bible app on your phone, or an audio Bible. Your prayer time might include a prayer journal, a prayer list, a prayer guide, or none of the above.

You can seek Jesus first throughout the day. Yes, seeking Him first thing in the morning sets your focus on Him for the day. But don't stop there. Seek Him first – before making that decision, before engaging in discipline, before the conversation with your husband.

This resolution will not come naturally. In our human nature, and amid spiritual opposition, our hearts seek independence. We're prone to think we can handle life on our own. Choosing to seek Jesus before seeking our own solutions requires commitment. We'll talk more on Day 1 about how to stay committed for twenty-one days because this resolution will require a supernatural resolve.

Our 21 Day Journey

These next twenty-one days are all about seeking Jesus first. Since seeking Him is not our natural response, we must train ourselves. We can create a habit by seeking Him daily during this intentional season.

Each day's devotion will include a short devotion, a prayer challenge, and a homeschool prayer focus.

The daily devotion will help you focus first on God's Word. Each short chapter highlights one verse or passage from the Bible. Reading the devotion is an opportunity to turn your attention to Jesus.

The prayer challenge may not always look like your current expectations for a time of prayer. Sometimes it's good to think outside our little box. Think of each challenge as a type of conversation starter. Use it as a springboard for a conversation with God. Questions are included to help you in prayer. The purpose of each challenge is to help you draw closer to Jesus.

The homeschool prayer focus aims to help you strategically pray through various areas of homeschool life. The goal of this portion is not to stir up guilt and regret, although it will likely uncover some difficult feelings. The goal is also not to fix the problem. You will probably be tempted to reorganize your school area, revise your family budget, or revamp your schedule. That's not the point.

The goal of the prayer focus is to seek Jesus first for a restful heart in each area of homeschool life. You will pray through each area in three ways:

EVALUATE

Is your heart currently restful in this area? Each day, you can identify how restful your heart currently is in that particular area. The 1-10 scale is not a grade or assessment of your heart or your competency. It's merely a tool to help you identify where you need Jesus to work in your life. You can also use it in the future to see where God has produced His peace in your life.

What are the cues of unrest in your heart? Cues of unrest could be waking at night worried about a certain issue, struggling with anxiety or depression, over-reacting to a particular situation, or striving to fix a problem. Well, those are some of my personal cues. We might share some, but yours might be different. Learn to identify your own cues of unrest so you can train yourself to seek Jesus quickly. Whatever your cues are, remember they can be a gift. These cues are a reminder to believe God can do far more abundantly beyond all you can imagine.

SURRENDER

Surrender your efforts to fix the problem. As you identify difficult areas, think about how you have attempted to solve things on your own. Your efforts are good, but you need Jesus. If you want true rest in your heart and your homeschool, hand your efforts to Him. Ask Him to do His supernatural work with the work you are doing in the natural.

Surrender your expectation of the outcome. Will you dare to believe God might want to do something different in your situation? Choose to trust that His plan for your family is good and He can mysteriously work all things for good. So release your expectations, let go of what you want, and trust His plan is better.

RECEIVE

Ask God to give you rest in the midst of the struggle. Yes, in the midst of it. Sometimes, He will outright deliver you from the situation. But usually, He has a better plan. He will walk with you through the struggle. His presence will give you strength and peace. His light can shine brightest in your darkness.

Ask God to give you guidance for ONE thing you can do to cultivate rest in each area. Yes, you can take a step toward rest. Just one step, though. One small, practical step. Our goal in these 21 days is not to fix all the problems. Our goal is to take on Jesus' yoke and learn from Him. Our journey toward rest is taken one step at a time.

Ten Tips for Success

A 21-day prayer focus is not a new idea. This book has been birthed from my past decade of life as I have joined my church's 21 Days of Prayer twice each year in January and August. This practice has transformed my life, but it most definitely has not been easy.

Prayer is difficult for me. Honestly, I really struggle to put words into prayer. I can say, "Dear Lord. . ." and my mind goes blank. In my devotion time, I'm tempted to simply read my Bible then move on with my day. Each 21-day season helps me reset my focus and retrain my habits, but it's always a fight for me to finish (truthfully, I've fallen short of twenty-one many times).

So if you make it through three days, then realize you're off course, you're not alone! Choose to get back up and try again. Your pursuit of Jesus will be worth the effort. He will transform your heart. He will transform your homeschool. Through my personal struggles, I've gleaned a few tips to help with the pursuit.

1. **Set a time and place.** Make a plan for when and where you will spend focused time with Jesus each day. If your children are young, go ahead and make a plan B and C.

2. **Start small.** If you're not currently in a habit of seeking Jesus each day, keep your plan simple. On Day 1, it might sound easy to set aside a full hour every day. Life might be different by Day 8, so plan accordingly.

3. **Invite a friend.** Find a friend to be your accountability partner for a few weeks. Check in with one another. Share your personal insights. Pray for each other.

4. **Join a discussion group.** Invite a group of friends to your home to seek Jesus together for restful homeschools. Or join an online discussion group with a group of other homeschool moms. Look for my next group at www.aimeesmith.com/21days.

5. **Write it out.** Even if you don't typically write a journal, try it. Write out your answers to the reflection questions. Write out your prayers. When you read them later, you can remember what God has done for you.

6. **Look up Scripture.** You will encounter many verses and passages from the Bible. Don't settle for receiving His Word through my words. Take time to pull out your Bible and read the full passage for yourself. Choose a verse or more to memorize.

7. **Give yourself grace.** If you miss a day, or many days, don't allow yourself to wallow in shame and despair. God is not looking for your perfection.

8. **Don't give up.** Give yourself grace, but don't quit and think you have to start over. If you miss some days, just start where you left off and keep going.

9. **Celebrate your growth.** On Day 21, read through your notes. Consider the work God has done in your life both in large and small ways. Celebrate even the small victories of rest in your heart and your homeschool.

10. **Repeat.** On Day 22, choose to continue your new habits to seek Jesus first. Eventually, you will need it again. Go through this book again at the beginning of the year, the

beginning of summer, the beginning of the school year, or whenever your heart and homeschool need a reset.

Bonus Tip:
Set a reminder to review this section on Days 7 and 14.

Let's Get Started

Are you ready to make the one resolution that can cultivate a restful homeschool? Decide now to seek Jesus first for 21 days. Seek rest in the person of Jesus. Receive rest as a gift in His presence. Cultivate rest through the journey of learning from Him.

As your heart grows more restful, so will your homeschool. I'm convinced the key to a truly restful homeschool is a momma committed to seeking Jesus first to cultivate a restful heart in herself.

Your resolution to seek Jesus first has power to transform your life. Allow Jesus to change your heart. Watch as He transforms your homeschool. This will be the year.

REFLECTIONS ON REST

Where are you seeking rest? How are you trying to create rest?

Write your own definition of rest. What do you really want?

How will you respond if becoming restful takes longer than you expect?

SCRIPTURE ABOUT REST

Look up the following verses about rest. Copy the verse. Jot down a few insights. You could look them all up at once or focus on one per day.

Micah 5:4-5a
Isaiah 30:15
Isaiah 26:3
Exodus 33:14
Philippians 4:6-7
Psalm 46:10
John 14:27
Psalm 62:1-2
Jeremiah 6:16
Psalm 55:18
Psalm 37:7

resolve

day one

SEEK JESUS FIRST. Easier said than done.

My alarm beckoned me to honor my commitment. I rolled out of bed, shuffled to the kitchen for coffee, and settled on the sofa with my Bible. I did it. I kept my commitment to seek Jesus first. Or so I thought.

An hour later, I woke to the baby crying. I realized I had failed again. I had been attempting to have my devotion early, every day, before my children woke. But keeping my commitment felt impossible.

There have been numerous similar scenarios throughout

the seasons of my life. I commit to twenty-one days of focused prayer, only to realize on day 17 that I stopped at day 4. I resolve to whisper a prayer before engaging my child in a discipline conversation, then realize I stepped out on my own. I decide in January this will be the year to truly seek Jesus first but fail way before February.

If you want a simple resolution, decide to make your bed each morning. Even that simple task can be daunting. Habits are difficult to change. For any new habit, distractions and disruptions will inevitably arise.

When you commit to seek Jesus first, however, the stakes are high. Don't underestimate the spiritual battle surrounding your choice to seek Jesus first. This decision has power to change the course of not only your homeschool but your entire life.

In the life of a homeschool mom, much opposition will arise to your resolution to seek Jesus first. Children will interrupt with true needs. Schedules and routines will shift. Sickness and spills will disrupt the good plan.

Moms, we're not the only ones. People throughout history have encountered spiritual and natural opposition to their attempts to seek Jesus. Throughout history, people have resolved to seek God amid immense opposition. Our struggles provide an opportunity to join them.

Daniel resolved to seek God in the midst of life-threatening opposition. King Darius, swayed by the leaders of the kingdom, issued a decree that no man was to make petition of anyone – man or god – besides the king himself. What did Daniel do?

"(Daniel) continued kneeling on his knees three times a day, praying and giving thanks before his God, as he had been doing previously." Daniel 6:10b

Even in the face of death, which he encountered first-hand in the faces of the lions, Daniel resolved to continue praying in pursuit of God. That's resolve.

Daniel's resolve was a habit. Three times a day, as he had been doing previously. Daniel's resolve remained because prayer was his habit.

What is your current habit with prayer, Bible reading, worship, and fasting? Continue doing well but consider taking one more step in your pursuit of seeking Jesus. The next twenty-one days will give you ideas of new habits you can incorporate into your prayer life.

Daniel's resolve was supernatural. The great stories of Scripture are not evidence of human strength. Resolve to passionately pursue Jesus daily, despite disruptions, requires supernatural resolve. We must decide, commit, resolve. But remember you cannot do this on your own. You must ask the Holy Spirit to give you the power of resolve.

Today's Prayer CHALLENGE:

WRITE DOWN YOUR RESOLUTION

Habits require a plan. Plans require a vision. Jesus Himself had a specific time and place, a plan, to talk with His Father (Mark 1:35). God instructed Habakkuk to record the vision and inscribe it on tablets (Habakkuk 2:2).

I don't have any Old Testament tablets lying around the house, but I do have some nice spiral notebooks. Reading my journals from previous twenty-day journeys inspires me to continue pressing in to a closer relationship with Jesus. The written record reminds me how much God has accomplished in my family. The written record helps me keep my commitment.

Your plan must be your own but be sure to write it down. Some will catch a few minutes during naptime. Others might wake an hour early. Just ensure your plan is doable *for you* for the next three weeks.

When will you pray? ________________________________

Where will you pray? ________________________________

Write out a prayer asking God for supernatural resolve.

____

____

____

Today's Prayer FOCUS:

YOUR PRIMARY AREA OF UNREST

Let's start where it hurts most. What area of your homeschool causes the most fear, anxiety, and exhaustion? What keeps you up at night? What thoughts, emotions, and situations are most overwhelming? What one struggle could lead you to quit homeschooling?

This is exactly where God wants to display His glory.

This is exactly where you need to seek Jesus first. As you resolve to seek Him for twenty-one days, begin by seeking Him in your most unrestful struggle. Spend a few minutes talking with Him about your greatest homeschool struggle. He loves you and wants to help you. He may not deliver you immediately, but His presence will give you rest as the struggle continues.

Rate the restfulness of your heart with your homeschool:

1 2 3 4 5 6 7 8 9 10

1=Anxious/weary/striving 10=Calm/trusting/restful

EVALUATE

What one area of your homeschool is most difficult?

____

____

____

Ask God to reveal any cues of unrest in your heart.

____

____

____

SURRENDER

Write out a prayer to surrender your efforts to fix the problem.

____

____

____

Write out a prayer to surrender your expectations of the outcome.

____

____

____

RECEIVE

Ask God for grace and rest in the midst of this struggle.

Ask God for *one thing* you can do to cultivate rest in this area.

NOTES

pause

day two

YOU COULD BE IN GRAVE DANGER. Homeschool moms, if we are not careful, we will trust in ourselves too much.

Most parents choose to delegate the responsibility of education, but you have courageously placed your child's education on your own shoulders. You research and read, plan and prepare. You possibly stay up too late at night searching for guidance for your homeschool's current source of struggle.

Your diligence toward responsibility could convince you

everything is under control. If not under control, then certainly a little more focus will take care of things. The danger sets in when you trust your understanding and knowledge and bear the weight of your homeschool. If you lean on your own understanding, you could forget Jesus.

> *"Trust in the Lord with all your heart, and do not lean on your own understanding. In all your ways acknowledge Him, and He will make your paths straight." Proverbs 3:5-6*

Any area of life where you are tempted to lean on your own understanding is exactly where you should pause. Pause long enough to remind yourself to acknowledge Jesus. You will not be able to see the path ahead of you, but Jesus can. Rather than lean on your own understanding, lean in to Jesus.

In order to trust in the Lord with all you heart, you must know Him. Knowing someone requires being close and spending time together. That's where prayer comes in. Prayer is the way your heart draws close to God's heart. Prayer helps you lean in to the One who can make your path straight.

Pause. Pray. Learn to trust Jesus. Then you will be ready to take a step of faith on His straight path.

With the non-stop lifestyle of homeschooling, however, I often find myself not stopping. Pausing seems impossible and certainly does not occur naturally. If we want to resist the temptation to trust in ourselves, we must fight for moments to pause.

Remember, however, that a pause is not a forever stop. You

stop activity for a moment or a season. Then you resume activity and take a step forward. After the pause, you can step forward in faith with lesson plans, character training, and schedule coordination.

Two simple practices are valuable tools to help in learning to pause: Fasting and Prayer Stops. Both are external pauses to train an internal response.

Fasting is a discipline of pausing something in your life. You stop something, but only for a season, to take your focus off yourself. It might be food, social media, any media, or numerous other possibilities. Regardless of what you pause, fasting is a reminder of your dependence on God alone. Fasting draws you closer to Him.

Prayer Stops are simple pauses throughout your day. Think of times during the day when you tend to depend too much on yourself. Set reminders on your phone for those times. Or choose set times of 9:00, 12:00, 3:00, 6:00. When the alarm chimes, pause and pray. Whisper a prayer of thanks. Talk with God about whatever is going on at that moment. Your current situation becomes your topic of prayer.

Fasting and Prayer Stops are excellent reminders of our potential danger. Pausing contains power to remind us to trust in God rather than ourselves. Pausing regularly can cultivate a restful homeschool.

Today's Prayer CHALLENGE:

PLAN TO PAUSE

Plan to pause for the rest of these twenty-one days. Remember: a pause is not forever. You can plan to pause by choosing to fast, setting prayer stops, waking early, or skipping a normal activity. Be sure your plan is doable, but don't be afraid to challenge yourself.

Will you choose to incorporate a fast for this season? What is something tangible you could choose to give up?

___

___

___

Will you set reminders for Prayer Stops throughout the day? What times?

___

___

How else might you plan to pause during the next twenty days?

___

___

___

Today's Prayer FOCUS:

YOUR OWN HEART

Momma, God loves *you*. Your heart is an important part of your homeschool. But more than that, your heart is simply important. God cares for you passionately in the midst of whatever is overwhelming you.

It is easy for moms to focus on everyone else and miss what's going on in themselves. If you will allow yourself to pause, you will be able to recognize the truth in your own heart.

What do you want Jesus to do for you? Not for your spouse, your children, your extended family, your neighbors, or anyone else. Yes, please pray for them. We will focus on others in the coming days. But right now, dream big for what you want God to do in your life during this season.

Seek Jesus first. He will give you rest.

Rate the restfulness of your heart in general:

1 2 3 4 5 6 7 8 9 10

1=Anxious/weary/striving 10=Calm/trusting/restful

EVALUATE

In what ways is your heart restful right now?

___

___

___

How is your heart not restful?

___

___

___

SURRENDER

How do you neglect caring for yourself while caring for others?

___

___

___

How do you expect others to meet your heart needs that only Jesus can fill?

___

___

___

RECEIVE

Write a prayer asking God for grace and rest today.

____

____

____

____

Ask God for *one thing* you can do to cultivate rest in your heart:

____

____

____

____

NOTES

____

____

____

____

____

____

____

anticipate

day three

JANUARY HAS A BAD REPUTATION. That's especially true in homeschool circles. The days are cold, dark, short. The fun activites of Christmas are over. The renewal of spring is still far away. Everyone stuck inside invites the unlovely side of togetherness.

Yet, it has become one of my favorite months of the year. Why? My church leads us in 21 Days of corporate prayer. After participating for more than a decade, this annual practice has changed my life. Even through the merriment of December, I anticipate my upcoming season of prayer and fasting. Yes, even the fasting part.

My faith has been fueled by seeing God respond to my prayers. My expectations grow each year as I trust He will be faithful and act on my behalf. His faithfulness in the past fuels my anticipation for the future. Year after year. Every January. Every August. Twenty-one days. Every time, He does something significant in my life. Wisdom. Direction. Calling. Provision. Healing. Vision. Restoration. Always significant and life-changing. A few examples:

2009 – God guided me to begin homeschooling. My husband was already convinced, waiting for me to receive confirmation of my true calling. God convinced me.

2010 - God gave me wisdom for physical healing. Through my minimal fast, He revealed foods that triggered major health problems.

2013 – I wasn't so faithful in my resolve to pursue Jesus daily, but He remained faithful. I look back and see how He poured out his blessing on me in the beginning of a difficult season.

2014 – Rest. My prayer list was long as I asked for help to accomplish all I thought needed to be done. Instead, God graced me with the gift of a season of rest.

2017 – The Holy Spirit, my Comforter, walked closely with me through the journey of caregiving for my mom and holding her hand as she stepped into eternity.

I'm always reminded of the time Jesus asked the blind man sitting by the road: "What do you want Me to do for you?" (Luke 18:41a)

I think He would ask you the same question. What do you want Jesus to do for you? What is that one area of your life that can only be rescued by Jesus Himself? What area is dead, dark, despairing? Perhaps it's a relationship. Financial strain. A struggling learner. Physical sickness. Emotional illness. Chaos and confusion.

Goal-setting cannot fix these problems. But Jesus can. Don't be afraid to ask Him. Don't hesitate to be specific. God knows everything about your life, but He wants to hear you ask. He wants you to trust him. He wants you to watch for Him to work on your behalf.

> *"In the morning, O Lord, You will hear my voice; in the morning I will order my prayer to You and eagerly watch." Psalm 5:3*

There is power in giving God the first. Morning is the beginning of the day. January is the beginning of the year. The beginning of the school year, the month, the holiday season, the week. Choose to seek Him at the beginning, and watch. Anticipate how He will act.

Today's Prayer CHALLENGE:

YOUR TOP PRAYER NEEDS

Write out Psalm 5:3 and Ephesians 3:20:

Order your prayer to the Lord, then eagerly watch for Him to respond. Ask, think, imagine, dream. Make it big. God can still do more. Far more abundantly beyond all you ask or think.

What do you want Jesus to do for *you*?

What do you want Jesus to do for your family?

Today's Prayer FOCUS:

FAMILY VISION

Anticipating what God will do for you is looking toward the future. You don't know how He will work, but you trust He will. However, God *has* given you creative ability to look toward the future. You can create a vision for your family and your homeschool.

Do you have a vision for your family's education? When your children graduate high school, what do you want them to know, think, be? What do you want them to say in memory of their homeschool years?

Is your vision written down? If yes, pull it out and review it. Discuss it with your husband. Talk with God about it. Ask if He wants you to change or add anything. Ask Him to help you if you are off track. If not, start small. Talk with your husband and write one sentence about why you homeschool. *I homeschool my children because...*

But not quite yet. Before writing, remember to *seek Jesus first.* Remember to pause. Receive His rest as you write your family vision. Expect Him to do more than you imagine.

Rate the restfulness of your heart with your vision:

1 2 3 4 5 6 7 8 9 10

1=Anxious/weary/striving 10=Calm/trusting/restful

EVALUATE

Do you have a family vision? How does it promote rest?

____

____

____

____

When you think about the future, what cues of unrest are in your heart?

____

____

____

____

SURRENDER

Write a prayer surrendering your efforts to make the vision happen.

____

____

____

____

____

RECEIVE

Ask God for grace and rest as you think toward the future.

Ask God for *one thing* you can do to cultivate rest with your vision.

NOTES

MY FAMILY VISION

A glimpse into my personal homeschool vision:

> *I homeschool because I enjoy being with my children and want to teach them day by day how to learn and how to live an abundant life.*

On the days I'm not enjoying them, my written vision serves as a reminder. Consider your family vision. If you're married, be sure to discuss your family vision with your husband.

I homeschool my children because...

____

____

____

When my children graduate high school, I want them to...

____

____

____

Memories I want my children to have of our homeschool...

____

____

____

____

believe

day four

WHAT IF GOD DOESN'T RESPOND? What happens when we pray for something big, but God doesn't give the answer we want? Maybe He seems silent. Maybe He does the exact opposite.

One of my prayer requests has remained at the top of my list for more than a decade. I have been asking God for complete, absolute healing from my chronic illness of rheumatoid arthritis.

Seasons of pain, fatigue, and despair overwhelmed me for years. In some seasons, I crawled up the stairs to tuck my children into bed. I knew God wanted more for my family, for me, so I cried out in desperation for His healing and deliverance.

He stayed silent.

In the midst of unanswered prayers, I learned to ask myself an essential question: *Will I believe God is still my Healer, even when healing is not my current reality?*

My homeschool prayers are no different. The same issues continue to creep into my prayers year after year. God has transformed much in our homeschool, but He stays silent in some details. I could doubt God is who He says He is for my children.

The essential question applies here too: *Will I believe God is who He says He is for my child, even when their current reality taunts otherwise?*

Prayer is not a Santa Claus list, as I have told my young children praying for new Legos. A focused season of prayer is not about getting what you want. It is about drawing closer to Jesus, seeking to know Him better, learning to trust Him more.

We encounter a difficult truth when drawing closer to God:

- If you want to know God as *your* Healer, you need a *sickness* to be healed.
- If you want to know God as *your* Provider, you must have a *need* to be provided.
- If you want to know God as *your* Comforter, you must experience a *hurt* to be comforted.

This difficult truth also applies to your children. Their struggles provide the opportunity to draw closer to Jesus.

Are you willing to make a difficult choice? Choose now, during the struggle, to believe God is who His Word claims He is.

"For I know whom I have believed and I am convinced that He is able to guard what I have entrusted to Him until that day." II Timothy 1:12

You can entrust your cares, burdens, and concerns to Him because He is able. You can especially entrust your children to Him. The more you know Him, the more convinced you will be that He is able to guard what and who you entrust to Him.

Believe God is who He says He is, even when you don't get what you want. Believe His promises are true, even when you don't see the reality in your current situation. Keep on praying, even when you feel like giving up.

Today's Prayer CHALLENGE:

CLING TO GOD'S NAME

God has many names in Scripture. You can find a list of some at www.aimeesmith.com/names-of-God. Each name reveals part of His nature like a multi-faceted prism. In each difficult situation of life, you can learn to know Him better according to that particular aspect. Ask Him to reveal Himself to you, draw you close to Himself, and convince you to trust Him more.

List the names of Jesus found in Isaiah 9:6

____

____

In what prayer of yours does God seem silent?

____

____

____

____

Choose one name of God to cling to. How does it apply to your unanswered prayer?

____

____

____

Today's Prayer FOCUS:

MARRIAGE OR SINGLENESS

"Weren't we praying for our homeschools?" you might ask. Yes, we are. Our focus will eventually be more specifically focused on school. But our relationships affect the restfulness of our hearts which affect the restfulness of our homeschools.

How is the restfulness of your heart in regard to your marriage relationship or lack thereof? This is an area many women feel God is silent as they pray for years about a specific issue in their marriage. That was true for me. One specific request for my marriage topped my prayer list for a decade. Now in hindsight, I see how I came to know God more closely as my Deliverer and our Restorer.

You may not see God answering your prayers yet, but you can trust Him with your marriage. Spend some time talking with Jesus about your marriage. Pray through the guide below. Ask Jesus for rest in this relationship.

Rate the restfulness of your heart in this relationship:

1 2 3 4 5 6 7 8 9 10

1=Anxious/weary/striving 10=Calm/trusting/restful

EVALUATE

How is your heart restful (or not) with your husband (or absence of one)?

___

___

___

How is any lack of rest displayed in your words or actions?

___

___

___

SURRENDER

Surrender your efforts to fix any problem areas.

___

___

___

Will you trust God with the outcome, even if it's different than your expectations?

___

___

___

RECEIVE

Write a prayer asking God for grace and rest in your marriage.

Ask God for *one thing* you can do to cultivate rest.

NOTES

worship

day five

MY ALARM WAS NOT MY FRIEND. I'm sure you understand the desire to snuggle back under the covers for just one more minute. I might not like it, but I never regret listening to that ringing friend.

During most seasons of focused prayer, part of my fast is skipping sleeping in. Getting up early. Making my prayer time priority each day. It's a way to deny my flesh what it wants in favor of strengthening my spirit.

I rolled out of bed and wandered to my Bible. My mind and heart were still not ready for my focused time of prayer. I read my Bible. God's Word is always good, but I still wasn't feeling it.

What finally made the difference? Worship. I turned up the music (in my headphones because this was not the time to wake my kids). I sang along. I willed myself to worship, to declare the truth of who God is.

Slowly, my heart joined in. My time of worship became enjoyable. I absolutely would not trade the time I had with the Lord that morning for more time under the covers.

Worship has not always been part of my quiet time. Over the years, however, it has become the heart of my daily time with God. I typically start my prayer time with one song of worship, then I keep the music playing while I pray. I move between talking with God about specific prayer items and singing along to focus my heart on Him.

As I step into action for my day, worship carries my prayer time through the day. After everyone is awake, I turn on the music in the kitchen. My kids can tell when it's a rough day for me because I cling to a song and play it repeatedly. They frequently grow annoyed with the repetition, but I tell them to trust me. It really is good for *them* for me to refocus *my* heart.

Perhaps worship is already part of your daily devotion routine. Perhaps not. Do you want to include a simple habit that could transform your heart? I highly recommend turning up the music.

"I will give thanks to the Lord according to His righteousness and will sing praise to the name of the Lord Most High."
Psalm 7:17

Worshiping the Lord should never be dependent on our feelings. Emotions are way too fickle. Our worship is to be *according to His righteousness*. His righteousness is true whether our feelings agree or not. Always.

I will give thanks.

I will sing praise.

Let's command our hearts to give thanks and to sing praise today. Our choice to worship is one more step in drawing close to the One who can bring rest to our souls. Worship can be one giant step toward a restful homeschool.

Today's Prayer CHALLENGE:

TURN UP THE MUSIC

Choose a worship song. Turn it on. Sing along. Yes, out loud. If your heart, like mine, needs a little help today to give God thanks and sing His praise, then turn up the music.

While you're worshiping, praise God for His name you chose on Day 4. Continue asking Him to reveal Himself to you. Talk with Him about the requests you listed on Day 3.

For ideas of my favorite worship songs, go to www.aimeesmith.com/worship.

What are your favorite songs to lead your heart to worship?

____

____

____

____

How might you incorporate worship into your daily routine?

____

____

____

____

Today's Prayer FOCUS:

YOUR STUDENTS' HEARTS

Do your students' attitudes lead your heart away from rest? Whining and complaining. Laziness and stubbornness. Pride and insecurity. Oh, these moments are the perfect opportunity to turn up the music. Worship will work wonders for both you *and* your children. Worship can draw all of our hearts toward Jesus.

Have you considered how the state of you own heart affects how you respond to the sinfulness of your children's hearts? How do you usually handle poor attitudes in your homeschool? You could give your *right* answer or your *real* answer. Honesty is crucial here.

Only the Holy Spirit can cultivate true heart change in our children, but He has given us the task of planting seeds for Him to grow. We must remember to seek Jesus first when training our children so we can begin with our own hearts in the right place. We certainly cannot handle this area of our homeschools alone.

Rate the restfulness of your heart with your students:

1 2 3 4 5 6 7 8 9 10

1=Anxious/weary/striving 10=Calm/trusting/restful

EVALUATE

How is your heart restful or not regarding your students' hearts and attitudes?

____

____

____

When your heart is not restful with them, what words and actions reveal the unrest in your heart?

____

____

SURRENDER

Are you trusting Jesus to transform your children's hearts or placing that burden on yourself? Will you choose to trust Him?

____

____

How has the Holy Spirit already used your efforts to lead your children to Himself?

____

____

____

RECEIVE

Ask God for grace and rest as you learn to trust Him to accomplish His work in your children.

Ask Him for *one thing* you can do to cultivate rest with your children.

NOTES

enter

day six

THERE IS NO BETTER PLACE TO BE. Years ago, a friend asked for my favorite verse for a framed print she made for me. The verse I chose:

> *"One thing I have asked from the Lord, that I shall seek: that I may dwell in the house of the Lord all the days of my life, to behold the beauty of the Lord and to meditate in His temple." Psalm 27:4*

For years, I prayed this Scripture repeatedly. I wanted to be *with* God, to dwell in His presence. I know that is the blessing of heaven, but I craved His presence now. Here on earth. Every day. I believed His presence would bring rest and joy to my heart.

"In God's presence, there is fullness of joy." Psalm 16:11

For years, I wondered if it really was possible. Surprisingly, answered prayers have not been the highlight of my focused times of seeking God in prayer. Rather, I have received that one thing I asked from Him long ago: *to dwell in His presence.* At the end of every 21-day prayer season, I realize I am walking in greater awareness of His presence in my life. Entering God's presence every day is becoming my reality.

Consider that it should not be that hard to be in God's presence since He is omnipresent. His presence is everywhere. Yet, I frequently realize I am walking alone. Has He left me? I can rest assured that no, He has not left me, because I have this promise: "Never will I leave you; never will I forsake you." (Hebrews 13:5 NIV)

Why should we seek to enter His presence when He is always with us? Because our hearts tend to isolate ourselves, to attempt this thing called life on our own. We are the ones who stray.

Do you recognize this same tendency to isolate yourself from His presence? If you have a relationship with Jesus, it is not hard to enter His presence every day. We can enter God's presence through thanksgiving and praise.

"Enter His gates with thanksgiving and His courts with praise. Give thanks to Him, bless His name." Psalm 100:4

Thanksgiving. Give thanks to Him. What has God done in your life? In your heart? In your family? Just as we teach our children, let's remember to say "thank you."

Praise. Bless His name. Take the name of God you are clinging to (from Day 4) and praise God for who He is, even while you are still waiting for Him to reveal Himself in that manner. Beyond that, praise God that His nature is so complex, one name is not sufficient. Praise Him for His many names.

Entering God's presence is more about growing in awareness that He is right here. Right now. With you. With me.

Enter God's presence as you grow in your awareness of Him. Grow in your awareness as you thank Him for what He has done and praise Him for who He is.

Today's Prayer CHALLENGE:

THANK AND BLESS FOR FIVE

Read all of Psalm 100. What stands out to you?

____

____

Thank God for five ways He has blessed you recently.

1. ____
2. ____
3. ____
4. ____
5. ____

Praise God for five of His names.

1. ____
2. ____
3. ____
4. ____
5. ____

Need ideas? Check out www.aimeesmith.com/names-of-God.

Today's Prayer FOCUS:

FAMILY CONVERSATIONS

Pray through the times your family talks with one another. Meals, driving, game time, read aloud time. While cleaning, cooking, playing. Proactive and reactive. All. The. Time. Are your conversations restful or anxiety-provoking?

One way to foster rest in your conversations is to thank and bless together. Keep a family gratitude list. Focus on blessing God's name together. Thank God for specific things you enjoy about one another.

If your heart is not restful about your conversations, ask God to reveal what leads to the unrest. Ask Him to lead your family toward rest as you constantly talk with one another. Ask Him to produce His fruit of love, kindness, and gentleness in all of your hearts.

Rate the restfulness of your heart with your conversations:

1 2 3 4 5 6 7 8 9 10

1=Anxious/weary/striving 10=Calm/trusting/restful

EVALUATE

How is your heart restful or not regarding the conversations in your home?

____

____

____

How does your heart respond during difficult conversations?

____

____

____

SURRENDER

Write a prayer to surrender your efforts to fix the trouble spots in your conversations.

____

____

____

How might your expectations be contributing to any frustrations you feel about the words used among your family?

____

____

____

RECEIVE

Ask God for grace and rest in your heart even when the conversations surrounding you are not restful.

Ask God for *one thing* you can do to cultivate rest in your conversations.

NOTES

invite

day seven

THE BLOOD OF JESUS IS OUR INVITATION. We enter God's presence through praise and thanksgiving, as we discussed yesterday, but it's only possible because God invited us into His presence. He invited us through the sacrifice of Jesus.

When Jesus sacrificed Himself on the cross, the veil of the temple was torn in two. Without Jesus, our sin keeps us separated from God the Father. Without Jesus, we cannot enter His presence. Jesus gives us access to God the Father.

"For through (Jesus) we both have our access in one Spirit to the Father." Ephesians 2:18

We have access to the God of the universe! We have access to respond to the invitation to enter His presence. God not only wants to offer us an invitation. God wants to receive an invitation from us.

My children sometimes create plans without me. They contrive a plan to visit a friend's house. Excitedly, they present the details to me. My response: "But we haven't been invited. We won't just show up with a suitcase and walk in."

It's the same with God. He wants us to invite Him into our lives. Because Jesus has invited us into God's presence through the cross, we can invite Him into each area of our lives, hearts, days, and homeschools.

Do you invite Jesus into every detail of your life? He wants to be with you in your parenting, your school, your work, your cleaning, your church, your hobbies. Every aspect of your life.

Do you invite Jesus into every area of your heart? He longs to help with the hurt, the anger, the anxiety, and the isolation. He desires to celebrate with your joy, your achievements, your dreams, and your blessings.

Do you invite Jesus into every moment of your day? He yearns to be with you as you wake, before everything else, throughout morning tasks, during lunch, in the midst of afternoon activities, amid the evening busyness, while you end the day and fall asleep.

Do you invite Jesus into every aspect of your homeschool? He desires to help with planning, researching, scheduling, teaching, correcting, guiding, assessing, struggling, and celebrating.

If prayer is about entering into God's presence, then it is also about inviting His presence into every area of our lives.

The Bible ends with Jesus' promise that He is coming quickly and the request that Jesus fulfill His Word and come.

"The Spirit and the bride say, 'Come.' And let the one who hears say, 'Come.'" Revelation 22:17a

What a glorious day that will be! But we don't have to wait. We don't have to wait for the physical return of Jesus to invite Him into every aspect of our lives. We can invite Him to come. Right now. Today. This moment.

Let us say: Come, Lord Jesus.

Today's Prayer CHALLENGE:

INVITE JESUS TO COME

What is one area of your life, heart, day, or homeschool where you are not including Jesus?

____

____

____

____

What is one area of your homeschool where you are striving alone?

____

____

____

____

Invite Jesus into these places.

____

____

____

____

Today's Prayer FOCUS:

FRIENDS and FELLOWSHIP

You might have learned by now that the stereotypical concern of socialization is not an issue for most homeschool families. However, homeschooling does have a risk of isolation. Even in the middle of a crowd, you can feel lonely. You might be craving an invitation for true fellowship.

In our early years of homeschooling, I felt this void. I prayed diligently for a friend for my son. God answered my prayer and blessed us with friends and fellowship far beyond what I imagined.

Relationships are not always easy. In fact, they're often downright impossible. When your momma heart is not restful about your family's friendships, it's a cue. You need to lean in to Jesus. Ask Him to provide friendships for yourself and your children. Ask Him to guide your fellowship with others.

Rate the restfulness of your heart regarding friendships:

1 2 3 4 5 6 7 8 9 10

1=Anxious/weary/striving 10=Calm/trusting/restful

EVALUATE

How is your heart restful or not about your family's friends?

____

____

____

Do you desire to be invited into closer friendships? Are you struggling with any current relationships?

____

____

____

SURRENDER

Ask God to provide the friends your family needs.

____

____

____

In what current relationship do you or your child need His guidance for more Christ-like fellowship?

____

____

____

RECEIVE

Write a prayer asking God for grace and rest with your friendships.

Ask God for *one thing* you can do to cultivate rest.

NOTES

admit

day eight

WHAT IS YOUR GREATEST WEAKNESS? Courage will be required to admit the truth.

Weakness, insecurity, failure, sin. I would prefer to not admit these about myself – to myself or to anyone else. Yet, my unwillingness to admit the truth does not change the truth. I have weaknesses, and they affect the state of my homeschool.

"Admit" is a multi-faceted word. "To admit" is "to concede as true or valid." To admit our weakness, we must acknowledge the truth. But Merriam-Webster goes a step further. "To admit" is "to make known, usually with some unwillingness." Yes, I'm typically unwilling to admit my weakness. Are you, too?

Yet, the verb *admit* has another definition: "to give entrance or access." Such is the meaning of "Admit One" on an event ticket. We have choice over what we admit into our lives, what we allow to enter our lives.

True, many circumstances enter our lives over which we have no control. As we discussed yesterday, though, we can choose to invite God's presence. We can choose to admit Jesus into every area of our hearts, every aspect of our lives, every moment of our days. These two definitions work hand-in-hand in our relationship with Jesus.

When we admit our weakness, we can admit His power.

When we concede the truth of our shortcomings, we can give Him access into our lives. When we acknowledge our wrong-doing, we can invite Him to enter our lives and change us.

> *"And He has said to me, 'My grace is sufficient for you, for power is perfected in weakness.' Most gladly, therefore, I will rather boast about my weaknesses, so that the power of Christ may dwell in me." II Corinthians 12:9*

Paul declared that he was content with his weaknesses and difficulties (II Corinthians 12:10). But he went even further than contentment. Boldly, Paul declared he would *boast* in his weakness.

Lack of follow-through. Unkind words to those I love. Insecurity and pride, strangely intertwined. Lack of wisdom in parenting. Inconsistency. Anxiety over medical procedures. Desire to get my own way. Yep, I'll admit all those.

Over time, however, I am finding Scripture really is true in the reality of daily life. As I admit the truth about who I am, I see miraculous, supernatural power at work in my heart. As I admit my need, I realize how much I need His power.

But I know I'm not the only one. In which weakness of yours would you like to see Jesus' power at work?

Power is perfected in weakness. Our weakness gives us access to the power of Jesus Christ, the power of the God of the universe. Perhaps our weakness isn't such a bad thing.

Today's Prayer CHALLENGE:

ADMIT WEAKNESS to ADMIT POWER

Write out II Corinthians 12:9-10:

____

____

____

____

Admit Your Weakness. Acknowledge the truth about your weakness. Be courageous enough to be specific. What area of sin, weakness, failure, or insecurity do you feel resistant to admit?

____

____

____

Admit Jesus' Power. First, acknowledge that He has power over all things. Then, invite Jesus in to give you His power in the area of weakness you just identified. Write out a prayer asking for Jesus' power in that area:

____

____

____

Today's Prayer FOCUS:

SCHEDULES and ROUTINES

One homeschool-related weakness of mine relates to our family routines. I thrive on routine. My family thrives on routine. But I struggle with inconsistency. I frequently tweak the plan. At other times, life disruptions pull us off course.

Routines, habits, schedules, and plans are good. But we cannot put our trust in them. We must seek Jesus first and trust him to lead us to rest in our schedules and routines.

A perfect plan is not the goal. Ask Jesus for one step to cultivate rest in and through your routines today. Receive His rest even if your routine continues to feel overwhelming. If you struggle, this is a perfect opportunity to admit your weakness and admit His power.

Rate the rest in your heart with your schedule and routine:

1 2 3 4 5 6 7 8 9 10

1=Anxious/weary/striving 10=Calm/trusting/restful

EVALUATE

Which are you trusting more for a restful home? Routine and order, or Jesus?

____

____

____

How can routines be helpful in cultivating rest while you trust Jesus?

____

____

____

SURRENDER

Write a prayer surrendering your efforts. Trust Jesus to accomplish His supernatural work as you work in the natural.

____

____

____

Could God have a better plan for your routine than you do?

____

____

____

RECEIVE

Ask God for grace and rest with your routine.

Ask God for *one thing* you can do to cultivate rest in this area:

NOTES

express

day nine

I WAS AN UNLIKELY CHEERLEADER. In fact, I was only a cheerleader because I attended a very small school. Expressiveness is not one of my top qualities. I'm not one to cheer and yell loudly at sporting events. I don't jump up and down with joy when I'm excited. Even though I feel strongly internally, I don't tend to show it on the outside.

But if I stay in my comfort zone as I worship and pray, I might miss out on something God has in store for me.

In college, I experienced an expressive atmosphere of worship that was new for me. My assumption was that it was the college culture. Years later, I learned otherwise. I was challenged to step out of my comfort zone, to express my inward joy outwardly as I worshiped and prayed.

I vividly remember the day I hesitantly, oh so hesitantly, raised my hand just a little during worship. I opened my hands, ever so slightly, during prayer.

I felt awkward and exposed. Yet something started to change in me. My uncomfortable step led me to realize God has more blessing in store for my heart than I can imagine.

I have no idea what your church experience is like. I have no idea what your comfort level is in expressiveness. But may I challenge you? Try something new as you express your love for Jesus today.

Scripture is full of instruction to express our worship.

- Clap – Psalm 47:1a "O clap your hands, all peoples."
- Shout – Psalm 47:1b "Shout to God with the voice of joy."
- Lift your hands – Psalm 134:2 "Lift up your hands in the sanctuary and bless the Lord."
- Kneel – Psalm 95:6 "Come, let us worship and bow down, let us kneel before the Lord our Maker."
- Sing – Psalm 149:1a "Praise the Lord! Sing to the Lord a new song."
- Dance – Psalm 149:3a "Let them praise His name with dancing."
- Be Still – Psalm 46:10a "Be still and know that He is God." (yes, even being still can be expressive)

Worship and prayer are intertwined. As you are pursuing God through this focused season of prayer, worship can be a beautiful part of the journey. To draw closer to the heart of God, you might need to try something a little bit uncomfortable.

All of those actions above? They're biblical. King David was a man after God's own heart. He blessed God by expressing himself in worship. In the Psalms, he calls us to do the same.

I want to be a woman after God's own heart, just like David. I decided to take God at His Word and try something a bit new in prayer and worship. I haven't looked back.

Will you try something new today as you pursue God's heart?

Today's Prayer CHALLENGE:

EXPRESS YOURSELF IN WORSHIP

Just try something new. Express outwardly the praise that is in your heart. Sit. Stand. Walk around. Kneel. Open your hands. Raise your arms. Clap. Sing. Shout. Dance. Draw. Be still.

Does this suggestion bring an uncomfortable feeling? Why?

____

____

____

Choose a verse from the previous page. Read the full chapter for context. Thoughts?

____

____

____

What new expression did you/will you try today?

____

____

____

Today's Prayer FOCUS:

RECORD-KEEPING

Ah, homeschool records: evidence that we really do what we say we do as home educators. Perhaps your records are for your state. Perhaps your records are for a local cover school. Perhaps your records are for transcripts for high school graduation and/or college entrance. Perhaps they are a collection of memories for yourself.

Regardless of the purpose, is your heart restful when you think about these records? Some feel unrest because they're not sure they are recording enough information correctly. Some fear disapproval from an outside authority. Some simply feel consistently behind.

If you are not at rest, take your cue to bring this area of your homeschool to Jesus. He even cares about the records.

Rate the restfulness of your heart with your records:

1 2 3 4 5 6 7 8 9 10

1=Anxious/weary/striving 10=Calm/trusting/restful

EVALUATE

What is the current status of your school records?

____

____

____

What are your current cues of any unrestfulness with records?

____

____

____

SURRENDER

Does trying harder help or leave you more frustrated?

____

____

____

Write a prayer surrendering your work of record-keeping to Jesus.

____

____

____

RECEIVE

If this is a struggle for you, ask God for grace and rest in the midst of this struggle:

____

____

____

Ask God for *one thing* you can do to cultivate rest in this area:

____

____

____

NOTES

____

____

____

____

____

____

____

____

____

pour

day ten

POUR OUT YOUR HEART LIKE WATER.

We had to buy a new refrigerator recently. I have never had a new fridge before, so I'm loving how sparkling clean it is. My kids' favorite feature, however, is the "autofill" water dispenser. Place a cup under the dispenser, press autofill, walk away, return to a filled glass.

Until the moment it malfunctions. Yep, less than a month after we bought it. Place a cup under the dispenser, press autofill, walk away, return to a waterfall and puddles.

Once the water starts pouring, it continues until acted on by an outside force. Pour water from a pitcher; it continues until you turn it back upright. Stopping the flow of water in a creek, stream, or river requires great effort.

So it is with my heart. I can hold so much inside I block a flood of waters. I don't always know why I bottle up so much. It's partially my personality, partially the result of a too-full schedule, partially fear of what I might find inside. But once I begin to pour out my worries and cares, a flood of thoughts and emotions begins to flow.

Unfortunately, our heart-pouring is often combined with frustration and anger. Sadly, it is often aimed at the people we love. Deceivingly, we convince ourselves that venting or blowing off steam is acceptable.

Do you ever have moments your heart can no longer contain it all and gushes a flood of emotions? Those moments are so close to a biblical principle, but if we're not pouring out our hearts to Jesus, we miss the point.

> *"Arise, cry out in the night at the beginning of the night watches;* ***pour out your heart like water before the presence of the Lord;*** *lift up your hands to Him for the life of your little ones who are faint because of hunger at the head of every street." Lamentations 2:19*

Jerusalem was being destroyed. The enemy was prevailing. Even children were dying. And God wanted His people to pour out their hearts.

Your children may not be dying, but your problems are real. There is a thief, an enemy of your soul, seeking to steal, kill, and destroy. You might feel as if you're slowly dying on the inside. There's a flood of troubles, and the dam will eventually break.

Why not choose a proactive pouring rather than a reactive bursting? Set aside a few minutes to pour out your heart to Jesus. Tell Him everything that's bothering and smothering you. He already knows, but He wants you to trust Him with it. Before the flood bursts on everyone around you, pour out your heart in the presence of the Lord.

When we cling to our troubles, we resist receiving the blessings God intends for us. If we will pour out our hearts in Jesus' presence, a beautiful thing happens. Our hearts have space for Him to fill.

Pour out your *wounds*, those ways your heart has been hurt by people. Choose to receive healing and restoration.

Pour out your *confession*, the ways your heart has strayed from God's ways in sin. Choose to receive forgiveness and His righteousness.

Pour out your *grief*, the losses you feel both big and small. Choose to receive His hope and promises.

Pour out your *frenzy*, that list of concerns threatening to drown you. Choose to receive His peace and purpose.

You can pray out loud, write a prayer in your journal, jot down a bulleted list. Just get all the stuff out of your heart. Direct the pouring to Jesus. Open space in your heart for Jesus to fill with His abundance of life.

Today's Prayer CHALLENGE:

POUR OUT YOUR HEART

Take a few moments to proactively pour out whatever is filling your heart. Relational wounds? Guilt and shame? Grief? Overwhelming tasks? Parenting struggles? School-time strife? Just get it all out of your heart. Pour out your heart to Jesus.

Today's Prayer FOCUS:

FAMILY MEALS

Yes, it's true, you're more than just teacher. Meal planner and chef are two of your extra hats to wear, and it's harder than in a school cafeteria. Meal plans, grocery shopping, meal preparation, and your actual time around the table (or standing at the counter!). When out of order, family meals can definitely lead you away from rest.

How does your heart respond to meal planning and meal time? Remember, our goal in these 21 Days is not to fix the problem. We're asking Jesus to transform our hearts and show us one small step toward rest.

Are you trying to create rest rather than allowing Jesus to accomplish His work in your family? Don't stop your efforts. Just remember to surrender those efforts to Him and ask Him to do His supernatural work as your do the natural work.

Rate the restfulness of your heart around family meals:

1 2 3 4 5 6 7 8 9 10

1=Anxious/weary/striving 10=Calm/trusting/restful

EVALUATE

How would a fly on the wall describe your family meal time?

How does your current routine for meal-planning bless your family and cultivate rest?

SURRENDER

How might you be seeking to create rest for yourself through pursuing, planning, and preparing family mealtimes?

Write out a prayer surrendering expectations of family meals.

RECEIVE

If meals are a source of unrest for you, write out a prayer asking God to give you rest with them.

Ask God for *one thing* you can do to cultivate rest in this area:

NOTES

intercede

day eleven

I DON'T ALWAYS LIKE TO PRAY. Even with a prayer guide in front of me, I can struggle to find words to say. Even with a list of prayer needs before my eyes, the needs can feel far from my heart. Even as I write about seeking Jesus first, my prayers can fall flat as He seems distant.

On the days an invisibile gap stands between you and God, remember this truth: Jesus fills the gap. He stands at the right hand of God the Father, even now, interceding for you.

"Christ Jesus is the one who died – more than that, who was raised – who is at the right hand of God, who indeed is interceding for us." Romans 8:34 (ESV)

To intercede is "to intervene on behalf of another, to speak to someone in order to defend or help another person." *Interceding* is standing in the gap between two other people. *Intervening* is intentionally stepping into that gap.

Early one morning as I was struggling to pray, conflict erupted between two of my children. The conflict involved a shared bedroom, one late-sleeper, exhaustion from being up too late, and Legos. Feel free to imagine the rest. The combination resulted in anger, hurt, and a gap between siblings.

They couldn't close the gap on their own, so I intervened. I intentionally stepped into the gap to comfort the hurt and calm the anger. I also interceded. I cried out to God that He would work in their hearts because that's a job Mom cannot accomplish. As I stood in the gap for them, I was reminded how Jesus stands in the gap for me.

Jesus stands in the gap for you, too. Because of His death and resurrection, the gap between you and God has a bridge. However, there's even more.

The Holy Spirit also intercedes for you. On the day you're not sure what to pray, or the day you're just not enjoying prayer, rest in Him. He intercedes when we don't know how to pray.

"In the same way the Spirit also helps our weakness; for we do not know how to pray as we should, but the Spirit Himself

intercedes for us with groanings too deep for words."
Romans 8:26

Jesus intercedes for us. The Holy Spirit intercedes for us.

God calls us to follow His example and intercede through prayer for others. Our world is full of people who need someone intervening on their behalf before God's throne. Jesus has given us, the Church, the privilege of standing in the gap for them.

He urges us to intercede for many people:

- Pray for believers (Ephesians 6:18)
- Pray for those who don't believe yet (II Corinthians 4:4)
- Pray for your enemies (Matthew 5:44)
- Pray for the sick (James 5:15)
- Pray for those in authority (I Timothy 2:1-2)
- Pray for your children (Lamentations 2:19)

Rest assured that Jesus and the Holy Spirit are interceding for you. Follow their example and intercede for someone else. Who do you know that needs you to stand in the gap, to intervene on their behalf?

Today's Prayer CHALLENGE:

STAND IN THE GAP

Read Romans 8:31-39. What difference does it make in your life knowing that Jesus is interceding for you? What else stands out to you in this passage?

____

____

____

Now back up and read Romans 8:26-30. How can you trust the Holy Spirit when you don't know what to pray? What else stands out to you in this passage?

____

____

____

Every person you encounter has a need. You can stand in the gap for them. Ask God who He wants you to intercede for today. Spend some time praying for the first person that comes to mind. Who will you stand in the gap for today?

____

____

____

____

Today's Prayer FOCUS:

EXTENDED FAMILY

You may or may not have extended family members in the middle of your school day. Either way, they certainly influence our hearts as moms who are trying our best to educate and train our children well. You might wrestle with disapproval from others over your choice to homeschool. You might experience ongoing conflict with family. Regardless of your extended situation, Jesus can bring rest to these relationships.

Relationships will always hold potential to be complicated. Sometimes, you need to seek restoration and reconciliation through conversation. Sometimes, your just need Jesus to give your heart rest in the midst of hard circumstances. Always, you can pray. As you pray for rest in these relationships, take the opportunity to intercede for your family.

Rate the restfulness of your heart with extended family:

1 2 3 4 5 6 7 8 9 10

1=Anxious/weary/striving 10=Calm/trusting/restful

EVALUATE

What is your biggest struggle with extended family?

___

___

___

How is your heart restful or not with your extended family? What are your cues of unrest?

___

___

___

SURRENDER

How are you trying to fix family problems in your own strength?

___

___

___

How will you respond if your expectations of extended family are never met?

___

___

___

RECEIVE

If this is a struggle, write a prayer asking God to give you rest.

Ask God for *one thing* you can do to cultivate rest with your extended family relationships.

NOTES

pursue

day twelve

WE'RE HALFWAY TO TWENTY-ONE. As much as I love a 21-day prayer challenge, I'm always surprised with the resistance I feel smack-dab in the middle. But you're hanging in there. Well done!

While driving on a road trip, the middle of the journey is typically the hardest. Anticipation and excitement fill the beginning. Somewhere in the middle, they fade into the background as the miles seem long. But toward the end, as the destination draws near, anticipation and excitement return.

A prayer journey can be the same. You have been intentional in focused prayer time each day. But this could be the time you need some determination to push through some weariness.

A determination to push through fuels your pursuit of Jesus. To pursue is "to follow and try to catch or capture someone or something, usually for a long distance or time."

Pursuing Jesus is not a one-time activity. It's all about daily pursuit for an extended period of time.

Have you been surprised by some of our daily Prayer Challenges? Perhaps some haven't look exactly like prayer to you, but they have all focused on pursuing Jesus. That's what prayer really is: drawing close to the heart of God.

Let's revisit the challenges you've taken thus far:

- Write down your resolution
- Plan to pause
- Write down your top prayer needs
- Cling to God's Name
- Turn up the music
- Thank and bless for five
- Invite Jesus to come
- Admit weakness to admit power
- Express yourself in worship
- Pour out your heart
- Stand in the gap

The intent of each challenge is to help you draw close to

Jesus because that is how to cultivate a restful heart.

Does your pursuit of God feel fruitless? Oh, I hope not! Even if you don't feel as if you're getting closer to Him, hang in there! Take God at His Word, and trust this promise:

> *"You will seek Me and find Me when you search for Me with all your heart." Jeremiah 29:13*

If seeking God is a game of hide-and-seek, you win! Because of this promise, you can trust your pursuit will be successful. Seek God, search with everything in you, pursue Him, and you will find Him. You will draw closer to Him.

Keep going. Keep pursuing. Continue chasing after God each and every day. Pursue Jesus.

Today's Prayer CHALLENGE:

REPEAT A CHALLENGE

Read Jeremiah 29:11-14. How can you seek and search for God with all your heart?

____

____

____

____

Which previous challenges have been your favorites?

____

____

____

____

How will you pursue Jesus today?

____

____

____

____

____

Today's Prayer FOCUS:

HOUSEHOLD ORGANIZATION

Household organization is where I most often misplace my search for true heart rest. I love having everything stowed neatly in its place even though that is rare in a house of six people. When our home is disorganized, my heart quickly strays toward an unsettled state.

Organization and order are important. We should serve our families with a labor of love to create a restful atmosphere. At times, however, I have learned we need to rest in the mess.

Only the Creator of our hearts knows our true need at the current moment. He will give you discernment in whether it is a time to work or a time to let the work wait. In order to know the difference, you must seek Him first.

Rate the rest of your heart with household organization:

1 2 3 4 5 6 7 8 9 10

1=Anxious/weary/striving 10=Calm/trusting/restful

EVALUATE

If your home environment were perfectly clean and organized, do you think you would truly be at rest?

Look for any cues of unrest when you think about your home.

SURRENDER

How do you attempt to create rest in your home's physical environment? Surrender any way you're seeking rest in cleanliness and organization *more* than in Jesus.

Do you have misplaced expectations in your house? Entrust them to Jesus.

RECEIVE

Ask God for grace and rest in your home environment if this is a struggle.

____

____

____

Ask God for *one thing* you can do to cultivate rest in this area:

____

____

____

NOTES

____

____

____

____

____

____

____

____

____

listen

day thirteen

MOM, ARE YOU LISTENING? Have you been guilty of having a conversation with your child without really listening to them?

Yeah, me too. As a homeschool mom, this is something I do way too often. Since I am constantly with my four children, constant noise and chatter abound around me. Being able to tune out the noise is sometimes a survival tactic for my introverted self.

However, I can tend to tune out their voices and miss

beautiful opportunities to connect with them. My cue is when one of them asks that question: "Mom, are you listening?" To really listen to them, I must shut out the noise, including the noise of my own thoughts, and focus on them.

I could hear the same question from God: "Daughter, are you listening?" To really listen to God and hear His voice, I must silence the voices around me. I must focus on Him.

Learning to listen to people takes practice. Listening skills are commonly taught to improve communication. Learning to listen to God's voice is no different. It is a skill that requires practice, so don't be discouraged if you feel like you don't hear from Him. You can learn!

Get to know your Shepherd. Sheep know their shepherd because he spends time with them. They know his voice and follow him. Jesus calls Himself our Good Shepherd (John 10:1-18).

To hear His voice, we must get to know Him by spending time with Him. That's exactly what we're doing through prayer and spending time in the Bible. How can you get to know Him? Talk to Him. Read His Word. Be still to shut out other voices. It takes practice.

Listen for the still, small voice. While fleeing for his life, Elijah heard God's voice. God's presence was not in the strong wind, the earthquake, or the fire. Rather, His voice came in the sound of a gentle blowing (NASB), a gentle whisper (NIV), a still, small voice (KJV). (Read the full story in I Kings 19.)

I've heard people say they wish God would give them guidance through a billboard sign or on a notecard. We often look for the burning bush revelation of His Word when we just need to be still and listen for His quiet voice.

Respond when you hear Him. When you instruct your child in a certain behavior, you expect them to listen *and* respond.

> *"Today, if you would hear His voice, do not harden your hearts, as at Meribah." Psalm 95:7-8 and Hebrews 3:7-8*

Meribah was the place where, after their miraculous Exodus, the Israelites grumbled, complained, and quarreled because they had no water to drink. God showed His power and provision by bringing water out of the rock at Horeb. (Exodus 17:1-7)

A hardened heart refuses to respond. If your heart is characterized by grumbling, complaining, and quarreling, then you will not hear God. In contrast, a softened heart is willing to receive whatever He has to say. The more you refuse to respond to God's voice, the less you will hear Him. The more you choose to respond, the more you will hear.

Let's not be guilty of having a conversation with God through prayer without really listening to Him. Spend time with your Shepherd to know Him better. Listen for His still, small voice. Respond when you hear Him. Seize your opportunity to connect with Jesus today as you listen to Him.

Today's Prayer CHALLENGE:

LISTEN FOR GOD'S WORD

Choose at least one Scripture we considered to study further to learn how to listen to God.

Read John 10:1-8. How can you learn to know your Shepherd's voice?

____

____

Read I Kings 19. How can you learn to hear His still, small voice?

____

____

Read Exodus 17:1-7. How are you sometimes like the Israelites when they grumbled at Meribah?

____

____

Be still a few moments. Shut out other voices. Ask God for a reminder of His Word. Listen. Write down any Scripture the Holy Spirit brings to your mind.

____

____

____

Today's Prayer FOCUS:

CURRICULUM

Curriculum choice is an easy way to see unrest among homeschool moms. Many of us tend to research options endlessly, question our decisions consistently, and change curriculum frequently. Curriculum includes books, resources, and supplies. But it's much more. A curriculum is actually a "course", a roadway to take our children from one place to another.

A common temptation is to believe the right curriculum will ensure homeschool success. But the right curriculum cannot offer true heart rest. Only Jesus can offer rest to your heart regarding your curriculum decisions. He certainly desires to be invited into this area of your homeschool. Curriculum choice is an ideal opportunity to practice listening to Him.

Rate the restfulness of your heart with your curriculum:

1 2 3 4 5 6 7 8 9 10

1=Anxious/weary/striving 10=Calm/trusting/restful

EVALUATE

How is your heart restful (or not) regarding your family's curriculum? Ask God to reveal any cues of unrest in your heart.

____

____

____

How might you be seeking rest in your curriculum rather than in Jesus?

____

____

____

SURRENDER

How do you strive to find the *right* curriculum? Choose to surrender your efforts and trust Him to give you guidance.

____

____

____

What expectations do you have of your curriculum? Choose to surrender them and place your trust in Jesus instead.

____

____

____

RECEIVE

If being restful with your curriculum is a struggle, write out a prayer asking God to give your heart rest.

Ask God for *one thing* you can do to cultivate rest in this area:

NOTES

gather

day fourteen

FOR YEARS, I MISSED THE BLESSING. I viewed 21 Days of Prayer as *my* thing. I woke early, spent time alone with the Lord, attended church prayer services. All by myself. Then a friend challenged me to include my children. Obvious, yet it seemed like a novel idea.

We began gathering together each morning (ok, not every single morning, but most of them) for a time of focused prayer. We watched our church's prayer service online. Then we prayed. Simple.

Praying together wasn't a new experience. We have prayed together for years, but honestly, it has been a struggle for me. Consistency is my nemesis. I know the good I ought to do, and I know first-hand the value of it, but I still neglect to be diligent. Even though it was a struggle, it wasn't a new experience. However, involving my children in our church's corporate season of prayer was new.

The blessing overwhelmed me one Saturday morning. Our entire family attended the prayer service at church together. My heart was overjoyed as I watched my children praying over other people's prayer cards. They were interceding for deep troubles. They interceded for children, the sick, broken families, prisoners.

Walking into church, there had been grumbles about not wanting to go. But as we left, they were singing a different story. One child commented on how fast the hour seemed to pass. Another one begged to go again at 6am on Monday!

After that corporate prayer experience, I wanted to write something based on this word: Gather. One of my sons climbed into my lap, and we searched the Scriptures for this word. We had such fun!

> *"For where two or more are gathered together in My Name, I am there in their midst." Matthew 18:20*

God created us for unity in the Church, in our families, in community with one another. He desires to be with us collectively. So let's gather together to pray.

> *"Wherever there is a carcass, there the vultures will gather."* Matthew 24:28 (NIV)

This verse, out of context, was especially fun for a young boy! But my personal favorite:

> *"Then Jacob called for his sons and said, 'Gather around me so I can tell you what will happen to you in days to come'. . . All these are the twelve tribes of Israel, and this is what their father said to them when he blessed them, giving each the blessing appropriate to him."* Genesis 49:1&28 (NIV)

Right before his death, Jacob/Israel gathered his twelve sons around him and blessed them. When I gather with others to pray – my children, my husband, my friends, my co-laborers in ministry – I want to follow Jacob's example and pray God's blessing over them.

Often, I need help getting started, so I simply pray a passage from Scripture. If you also need a little help, here are some verses to get you started.

Write out the verses, including your children's names. Gather your children. Pray a blessing over them. I'm giving an example of the first one with my children.

Today's Prayer CHALLENGE:

GATHER YOUR CHILDREN

Write out Numbers 6:24-26, including your family's names: *The Lord bless you and keep you, Aron; the Lord make His face shine on you, Jackson, and be gracious to you, Malyn; the Lord turn His face toward you, Micah, and give you peace, Caleb.*

____

____

____

____

____

Repeat with Ephesians 3:14-21

____

____

____

____

____

____

____

Now gather your children together around you and pray this blessing over them out loud.

Today's Prayer FOCUS:

SIBLING RELATIONSHIPS

As you gather, you might encounter conflict or squabbles. Well, maybe not in your family, but that tends to happen around here. As we have journeyed through various areas of homeschool life that can be unrestful, I keep thinking we've hit my hardest personal struggle. Then we move to the next day.

I'm there again. Perhaps sibling relationships are most unrestful for me. The fussing, pestering, and bickering drives me crazy. Honestly, some days I completely lose control of my response. Yes, my husband and I are intentional in character training and consequences for wrong behavior. But we cannot change our children's hearts toward one another.

Heart change is the work of the Holy Spirit. Love, peace, and patience are among the fruits *He* produces. Not me. My role is to stand in the gap for their relationships and ask God to do what only He can do.

But their hearts aren't the only ones who need changing. My heart also needs the touch of the Holy Spirit. My non-gentle response is another cue I need to draw closer to Jesus. Let's evaluate, surrender, and receive His rest even before His work is complete in them.

Rate the rest in your heart with sibling relationships:

1 2 3 4 5 6 7 8 9 10

1=Anxious/weary/striving 10=Calm/trusting/restful

EVALUATE

How do you respond to sibling problems in your home?

___

___

___

What does your external response reveal about your heart?

___

___

___

SURRENDER

Are you trying to be your children's Savior? How do you try to rescue them in a way only Jesus can?

___

___

___

How might your expectations of their relationships be unrealistic?

___

___

___

RECEIVE

If your heart strays from rest in response to sibling relationships, write out a prayer asking God to give you grace and rest.

____

____

____

Ask God for *one thing* you can do to cultivate rest in this area:

____

____

____

NOTES

____

____

____

____

____

____

____

____

declare

day fifteen

STILL STRUGGLING WITH WORDS TO PRAY? You decide to pray for five minutes, but after thirty seconds you're out of ideas. You hear of others praying for an entire hour, and it sounds impossible.

Yesterday, we gathered our children together to pray a blessing over them. We used God's Word as our template of what to say, but there are more ways God's Word is our guide in prayer. Praying Scripture provides assurance we're praying according to God's will and helps us when our minds seem empty. One of my favorite ways to use God's Word as a prayer guide is to declare the truth of His Word.

In declaring God's Word, we can again follow the example of Jacob/Israel. Years before gathering his sons to his deathbed, he encountered his brother in a potentially disastrous circumstance.

Jacob and Esau were years beyond the circumstances of betrayal, deception, and the stolen birthright. At the urging of his mother, Rebecca, after his father, Isaac's, death, Jacob had moved far away. Now he was returning home with his wives and children. After his conflict with Esau years before, he did not know what to expect from his brother. He feared for the safety of his family.

So he prayed.

> *"Deliver me, I pray, from the hand of my brother, from the hand of Esau. . . For You said, 'I will surely prosper you and make your descendants as the sand of the sea, which is too great to be numbered.'" Genesis 32:9, 11 & 12*

For You said. Jacob remembered what God had previously promised Him. His plea for protection rested on the foundation of God's Word. He believed the promise was true simply because God had said it. So he declared that truth.

What has God said to you? It's not a trick question. Open your Bible and start reading. His Word is right there in front of you. Ask Him to remind you of the Scripture you already know.

Then declare the Truth from His Word. Need some help to get started?

God, I'm afraid. I feel alone in my battle. ***But You said,*** *"Be strong and courageous. . . for the Lord your God is with you wherever you go." (Joshua 1:9 ESV) Thank You for never leaving me alone. Give me Your strength and help me remember to trust You are with me.*

God, I can't see how any good can come from this situation. My heart hurts; my child's heart hurts. ***But You said,*** *"God causes* ***all things*** *to work together for good to those who love God." (Romans 8:28) All things. Even this. But only You can accomplish good in this. Help me trust You.*

Just remember: these promises are true if you have a true relationship with Jesus. Not sure if you have this relationship? Check out www.aimeesmith.com/relationship-with-Jesus or email me at aimee@aimeesmith.com.

Today's Prayer CHALLENGE:

DECLARE TRUTH

Use the following prompts to declare God's truth in your current situation.

Unsure of the future? God's plans for you are good. Write a prayer declaring Jeremiah 29:11.

____

____

____

Feeling like you've stalled in your spiritual growth? God will complete the work He started in you. Write a prayer declaring Philippians 1:9.

____

____

____

Wrestling with guilt over your failures? Your sin is completely forgiven in Jesus. Write a prayer declaring Psalm 103:12.

____

____

____

Today's Prayer FOCUS:

FINANCES

A common area of struggle for families is finances. It's another area that's not directly part of our homeschools but absolutely affects the atmosphere of our schools. If our finances are out of order, the unrest in our hearts can lead our homes away from rest.

If finances are a struggle, it's time to cling to Jehovah-Jireh, God our Provider. Your need is an opportunity for Him to reveal Himself in this way.

Financial struggles are also a wonderful opportunity to declare God's Word. "And my God will supply all your needs according to His riches in glory in Christ Jesus." (Philippians 4:19) "I (God) will bless her with abundant provisions." (Psalm 132:15a NIV)

Remember: Our goal during this 21-day challenge is not to fix every problem area. Our goal is to identify areas of unrest (weariness, worry, striving, fear, etc.). These are cues for us to draw closer to Jesus, to ask Him to give our hearts rest even during the struggle.

Rate the restfulness of your heart regarding your finances:

1 2 3 4 5 6 7 8 9 10

1=Anxious/weary/striving 10=Calm/trusting/restful

EVALUATE

What is your heart's attitude about your finances?

___

___

___

What do you believe about God as Jehovah-Jireh, your Provider?

___

___

___

SURRENDER

Are you trusting yourself or expecting your spouse to fix the problem at the expense of trusting in Jesus?

___

___

___

Is there a specific action you know you've been neglecting to be a good steward? (No despair– confess and thank God for His forgiveness; then take a step of obedience.)

___

___

___

RECEIVE

If finances are a difficult area, write out a prayer asking God to give you grace and rest.

____

____

____

Ask God for *one thing* you can do to cultivate rest in this area:

____

____

____

NOTES

____

____

____

____

____

____

____

____

____

succeed

day sixteen

THE LESSON PLAN BOOK DECLARED ME A FAILURE. In summer, those well-constructed plans had seemed perfectly doable. This was the year I would follow-through. This was the year we would be consistent. This would be the year of visible success.

By October, however, the pages taunted my weary heart with another story. Boxes remained unchecked. Books on the planned list still sat in a stack. Math lesson #27 had been bumped forward an uncounted number of days.

Some of my excuses were valid: a stomach virus invasion, a

dying fridge replacement, and family hospital visits. But deep inside, I knew that wasn't the full story. Many days, we just didn't get around to doing what I intended to do. So those blank planner pages revealed the perfectly undone plan. Failure stared me in the face once again.

You, too, exert great effort in your plans for the year. You invest your soul and energy into numerous tasks each day. Even today, many items on your task list await you. You want to succeed in each one, especially when the plans are for your children.

One simple truth ensures success in everything you do.

"Commit to the Lord everything you do. Then your plans will succeed." Proverbs 16:3 (NIRV)

You might recognize this verse from other versions which say, "Your plans will be established." But I love the simplicity of the New International Reader's Version, written for early readers: *Your plans will succeed.*

If you will commit to the Lord everything you do today – every goal, every lesson, every task – these plans will succeed.

Does this mean your plans will always look successful? Not necessarily. This is a matter of trusting that God, in some mysterious way, makes all things work together for good (Romans 8:28). It is a matter of trusting He is sovereign over all, even in what feels like failure.

The key to success is to commit. Commit means "to put into charge or trust; to entrust." Put Jesus in charge of everything you plan to do today. Entrust to Him the outcome of all your efforts.

That feeling of failure in October? A greater truth was at work. During my summer planning, I had committed our year to the Lord. The result? What I viewed as failure was a beautiful success still in progress.

By May, I gained a new perspective. We were still behind in math lessons, off-course in our read-alouds, and under-achieving in checkmarks. The year as a whole, however, was a success. My children had gained knowledge and grown in understanding. Their character had taken steps of development. We had enjoyed time together as a family.

Whatever you commit to Him will be a success, even if it ends up feeling like a failure.

Today's Prayer CHALLENGE:

COMMIT TODAY'S AGENDA

When have you seen God work His success in a plan you thought had been a failure?

____

____

____

In what plans have you *not* been trusting the Lord?

____

____

____

What is on your agenda today?

As you write a list of today's plans and tasks, pray: "Jesus I commit _______ to You. I trust You to bring success in this plan."

____

____

____

____

Today's Prayer FOCUS:

HOUSEHOLD CHORES

Does the pile in the kitchen sink lead you toward feelings of failure? An insurmountable mountain of laundry? A ring around the toilet? The list of never-ending, messy battles is a common source of unrest in homeschool moms' hearts.

Sure, these are menial tasks that simply require your diligence to do the hard work. But with the many hats you wear, even the simple tasks are daunting.

Success in household chores doesn't necessarily require a pristine floor where you could serve dinner. Jesus has a deeper dream for your heart than for your toilet. He wants to give you rest in these most menial of chores. You can rest with your daily, unending chores by evaluating and surrendering them in prayer.

Commit to the Lord *everything* you do. Even mopping floors and scrubbing toilets.

Rate the restfulness of your heart with household chores:

1 2 3 4 5 6 7 8 9 10

1=Anxious/weary/striving 10=Calm/trusting/restful

EVALUATE

Which common household task is causing you the most unrest today?

___

___

___

Do you somehow think your heart would be restful if you could just get the mess under control?

___

___

___

SURRENDER

Are you entrusting your heart to Jesus in the midst of the mess?

___

___

___

What expectations of your household can you surrender?

___

___

___

RECEIVE

If this is an area of unrest for your heart, write out a prayer asking God to give you grace and rest.

Ask God for *one thing* you can do to cultivate rest in this area:

NOTES

calibrate

day seventeen

WHAT DOES "CALIBRATE" HAVE TO DO WITH PRAYER?

For me, a little bit of everything. This one word describes what occurs in my life during an intentional season of prayer.

Calibrate – "to standardize by determining the deviation from a standard so as to ascertain the proper correction factors." Calibration is a process of adjustment and alignment. You determine how far something is from the standard then make effort to correct the difference.

Scales are calibrated to correctly measure weight.

Thermometers are calibrated to accurately measure temperature. Printers are calibrated to properly disperse ink onto paper. Rifle scopes are calibrated to accurately hit where aimed. A compass is calibrated to ensure it points to true north.

For these devices to function properly, they must be calibrated. They must be realigned to the standard. They must adjust to the truth. The instrument must be changed to measure a true value. The standard does not adjust to the instrument.

Calibration can be a matter of life or death. Small airplanes rely on altimeters to measure altitude by determining barometric pressure. If the pilot does not calibrate the altimeter before take-off, he will receive false readings of altitude while in the air. A false reading can lead to a crash.

Your life is no different. In order to function how God desires, you must calibrate yourself. You must realign to God's standard. You must adjust to Truth. You must allow yourself to go through a process of being changed. Consider three areas of life to calibrate and realign to God's Word.

Calibrate your mind.

"Do not be conformed to this world, but be transformed by the renewing of your mind." Romans 12:2

Transformation begins in your mind. The messages our minds receive from our culture are overwhelming. We live in a time of information overload, so our minds need constant renewal. We renew our minds in God's Word, but this requires spending time in His Word. During this journey, we have intertwined Scripture with our prayer. We have been renewing our minds.

Calibrate your actions.

"Therefore, to one who knows the right thing to do and does not do it, to him it is sin." James 4:17

Ouch! For me, it's the little things. I know the value of seeking first God's kingdom (Matthew 6:33), but I allow other things to take priority. Over the past eighteen days, however, our actions have been calibrated. We are realigning ourselves with obedience to seek Jesus first. Our habits are being reset. Our actions are being realigned.

Calibrate your heart.

"Draw near to God and He will draw near to you." James 4:8

Our hearts are deceitful (Jeremiah 17:9), so we cannot trust them. Only God understands our hearts, so we must draw close to Him for our hearts to change. You will not realize how far off course you are unless you draw near enough to see His Truth.

In the course of everyday life, it is easy to get off course. We typically do not notice how we have strayed. That is why we need these twenty-one days. This intentional season reveals where our lives deviate from the Standard. It is an opportunity to rebuild habits that help us function according to God's Truth.

Today's Prayer CHALLENGE:

CALIBRATE YOUR LIFE

Read Romans 12:1-2. What thoughts in your mind need renewal?

____

____

____

Read James 4:17. What actions do you know you should be doing? (remember God offers grace!) Make a choice for a small step of obedience.

____

____

____

Read Jeremiah 17:9 and James 4:8. Remember the outward actions you listed above flow from your heart. How are you drawing close to God so He can transform your heart?

____

____

____

Today's Prayer FOCUS:

EXTRA-CURRICULAR ACTIVITIES

This is an area where my heart certainly needs constant calibration. Our family's activity level tends to swing on a pendulum. We're over-committed for a season, so we pull way back. Each season of the year is an opportunity to consider whether we are making wise decisions with our activities.

As we near the end of our twenty-one days, this is a perfect opportunity to evaluate the extras we're including in our family life. Sometimes, unrest in our hearts is a cue something needs to change. Other times, our activities are exactly what we should be doing to lead our families toward Jesus, and He offers you peace in the midst of them. Only He can show you the difference.

Rate the restfulness of your heart with extra activities:

1 2 3 4 5 6 7 8 9 10

1=Anxious/weary/striving 10=Calm/trusting/restful

EVALUATE

What are your current extra-curricular activities? What could be causing any unrest you're feeling?

___

___

___

Do you need to change some activities, or do you need Jesus to give you rest as you continue them?

___

___

SURRENDER

Are you trying to create a restful heart, or are you trusting Jesus to give you rest? Or are you just trying to survive, thinking rest is impossible, as you go from one activity to the next?

___

___

Would your heart be truly restful if you had fewer activities? Or would there still be a void only Jesus can fill?

___

___

___

RECEIVE

If this is an area of unrest for your heart, write out a prayer asking God to give you grace and rest.

Ask God for *one thing* you can do to cultivate rest with your activities.

NOTES

---

approach

day eighteen

BOLDLY APPROACH GOD'S THRONE. Really? Approach the God of the universe with boldness? That's rather presumptuous. Yet, it's exactly the instruction we receive in the Bible.

> *"Therefore let us draw near with confidence to the throne of grace." Hebrews 4:16*

In my human nature, my personality is not characterized by boldness. My tendency is more toward fear, insecurity, and timidity. In college, I set a goal to speak up at least once during a semester-long class. At restaurants, I will accept the wrong order rather than pointing out the mistake. I don't even like making phone calls to schedule appointments.

Earlier in my life, this timid tendency would spill over into my prayer life. My prayers were hesitant. I resisted asking for fear I would be disappointed if God did not answer. My insecurity often prevented me from approaching God Almighty.

Besides, I didn't really know what to pray other than to ask God to help with problems. That felt selfish. So I often remained quiet.

Does this hesitancy and reluctance feel familiar? Perhaps you, like me, can be timid and half-hearted in your prayers. Perhaps some of our prayer challenges have felt a little awkward. Perhaps you still doubt whether you really deserve to have a conversation with God Himself.

There is hope for us! Before following the instruction to draw near to God with confidence, we must look back at the verse prior to Hebrews 4:16.

> *"Therefore, since we have a great High Priest who has passed through the heavens, Jesus the Son of God, let us hold fast our confession. For we do not have a High Priest who cannot sympathize with our weaknesses, but One who has been tempted in all things as we are, yet without sin."*
> *Hebrews 4:14-15*

Jesus is your High Priest, the one who stands in the gap for you (as we discussed on Day 11). He understands your weakness, and He is the one who gives you access to God Almighty.

Because of Jesus, you can approach God boldly. You have no need to fear because your access to God Almighty is through Jesus who became man.

Today's Prayer CHALLENGE:

APPROACH WITH BOLDNESS

What is your perspective when approaching God in prayer? Confident? Timid? Empty?

____

____

____

Look back through the previous seventeen days. Which three challenges are your favorites?

____

____

____

Choose one previous challenge to repeat today. This time, knowing Jesus gives you access to God, approach Him a bit more boldly than last time.

____

____

____

Today's Prayer FOCUS:

TECHNOLOGY

Oh, this is a big one! I cannot even begin to describe the potential unrest technology can bring into our homes. However, we also cannot underestimate the potential benefits of technology.

Parents of the current age are figuring this one out on our own. We do not have a generation of mentors who have "been there, done that." This is certainly an area we must trust in the wisdom of the Holy Spirit.

I have no perfect answers for us. My husband and I are struggling through finding balance. We aim to tame the technology monster while training our children (and ourselves) to utilize the value of technology to serve others.

We may not have perfect answers, but there's one thing I do know: Jesus can bring our hearts to a place of rest – even with technology.

Rate the restfulness of your heart regarding technology:

1 2 3 4 5 6 7 8 9 10

1=Anxious/weary/striving 10=Calm/trusting/restful

EVALUATE

What are some benefits your family receives from technology?

____

____

____

In what ways is your heart unrestful with technology? How could this unrest be a cue for you to draw near to Jesus?

____

____

____

SURRENDER

How are you trying to tame technology in your home?

____

____

____

Will you surrender these efforts and ask Jesus to work through them?

____

____

____

RECEIVE

If technology is an area of unrest for you, write out a prayer asking God to give you grace and rest.

___

___

___

Ask God for *one thing* you can do to cultivate rest with technology.

___

___

___

NOTES

___

___

___

___

___

___

___

___

surrender

day nineteen

IS YOUR HOMESCHOOL MORE RESTFUL YET? Is your heart growing more restful? Yes? Praise the Lord! No? No despairing. He is not finished with you yet!

You probably picked up this book with the hope of experiencing a more restful homeschool. Along the way, however, you might have experienced moments of discouragement and frustration.

You have spent the past eighteen days with a commitment to seek Jesus first. Each day's prompts have been different intentional ways to seek Him, to draw near to Him, to cling to Him. You have been praying through various areas of homeschool life.

Perhaps you expected almost magical changes. Remember our goal in this short season was not to fix all the problems. Our goal has been to seek rest for our hearts that only comes from being near Jesus.

We are seeking rest in the person of Jesus. We are receiving rest as a gift from Him. We are cultivating rest through a journey of seeking Him first. As our hearts as moms become more restful, our rest will slowly permeate our families' homeschools.

But after these eighteen days, it is possible your heart is no more restful than on day one. Frustration and despair could be tugging at your heart because you don't feel closer to God than in the beginning. You might feel an invisible wall you cannot break through to draw closer to Jesus.

Are you holding on to something that has become a barrier between you and God? Expectations, dreams, plans, hurts, disappointments, idols, guilt, pride, control, anger, unforgiveness. When you stubbornly hold on to any of these, they can prevent you from enjoying God's presence.

Today, you can surrender whatever might be creating a barrier between you and God. Trust that God's plan for you is good. Let go of controlling the outcome. Release your expectations of the situation.

Surrender is an odd verb – exactly how do you do it? My heart cries for a simple 3-step plan, but it's not so simple. In my life, surrender is usually messy. It involves tears, a breaking point, and pouring out my heart to God. Sometimes, being the list-maker I am, I journal a bulleted list of everything weighing heavy on my heart. Sometimes, I write out a prayer and allow it to sound less-than-beautiful. Surrender always involves an honesty I would prefer not to admit.

In those moments of surrender, I inevitably realize three truths: God calms my overwhelmed heart. God rejoices over me. God is victorious.

> *"The Lord your God is in your midst, a victorious warrior. He will exult over you with joy, He will be quiet in His love, He will rejoice over you with shouts of joy." Zephaniah 3:17*

Oh friend, let go of that barrier and rest in His embrace. He longs to rejoice over you. He desires to calm you with His quiet love. He wants to be your victorious warrior.

You've experienced this moment with your child. He stops fighting and clings to you for a hug. She releases the dangerous item and allows you to protect her. You long for their moment of surrender because you love them dearly, because you have wisdom they do not, because you long for them to be close.

So surrender your barrier today. Stop fighting and rest in His embrace. Know His love is perfect. Cease striving and know He already rejoices over you. Rest knowing Jesus is a warrior who brings you victory.

Today's Prayer CHALLENGE:

SURRENDER YOUR BARRIER

What is still creating a barrier between you and God? (anger, guilt, expectations, disappointments, regrets, unforgiveness)

____

____

____

____

____

Write out a prayer of surrender to let go of your control and expectations.

____

____

____

____

____

____

____

Today's Prayer FOCUS:

LIFE DISRUPTIONS

One area constantly requiring surrender is in life disruptions, those times when we must let go of our carefully constructed plans and agenda.

My homeschool story is a series of interruptions and disruptions. In month three of our first year, I was hospitalized for over two weeks with complications in my fourth pregnancy. My nice little lesson plan, even my plan B for when baby arrived, was thrown completely off course.

Over the years, the disruptions just continued. Short-term illness and long-term illness. Celebrations and tragedies. Quick crises and drawn out trials. No matter the cause, when my plans are interrupted, my heart is tempted to stray from rest. You, too?

Jesus can give your heart rest by changing your perspective of the disruptions. These apparent interruptions can actually become part of your family's curriculum – the course set before you to build your character and lead you toward deeper trust in God.

Rate the rest in your heart with current disruptions:

1 2 3 4 5 6 7 8 9 10

1=Anxious/weary/striving 10=Calm/trusting/restful

EVALUATE

What disruptions have you experienced recently?

___

___

___

What are your cues that your heart is not restful?

___

___

___

SURRENDER

How are you trying to fix the problems on your own?

___

___

___

What are your expectations with these disruptions? Will you surrender them to Jesus?

___

___

___

RECEIVE

If disruptions are currently frustrating your heart, write out a prayer asking God to give you grace and rest.

____

____

____

Ask God for *one thing* you can do to cultivate rest with disruptions.

____

____

____

NOTES

____

____

____

____

____

____

____

rejoice

day twenty

LET'S REPEAT OUR QUESTION FROM YESTERDAY. Is your homeschool more restful yet? Is your heart feeling a bit closer to Jesus than on day one?

Yes? Then it's time to rejoice!

Celebrate all that Jesus has done for you. Thank Him for the ways He has answered your prayers. Write down a reminder of how He has revealed Himself to you. Reflect on what you have learned. Consider a new way of seeking Him you have begun to practice. Rejoice that He is able and that He acts on your behalf.

But wait, maybe you're still not feeling much different than on day one.

No? Not feeling restful? It's still time to rejoice!

You see, celebrating God's goodness is not dependent on what is going on around or in us. Rejoicing in God is based on Who He is, and He never changes. Sometimes we must make an intentional choice.

Sometimes, you must choose to rejoice. You might find it is in the dark times when you can truly appreciate Him for the God He is.

> *"The people who were sitting in darkness saw a great Light, and those who were sitting in the land and shadow of death, upon them a light dawned."* Matthew 4:16

If we will open our eyes in the darkness, we can see the Light brighter than at other times. In order to see in these times, we must choose to open our eyes. We must choose to see Light in the apparent darkness.

Celebrating, giving thanks, rejoicing. These are all ways we force our eyes to see truth. We focus on the good God is doing despite the heaviness of circumstances around us. Rejoicing helps us to see.

This choice to rejoice requires a stubborn resolve. Our resolution of the past twenty days to seek Jesus first is helping build that type of resolve.

You can purposefully choose to rejoice today:

Even if the diagnosis lingers.

Even if the grief hangs heavy.

Even if the conflict persists.

Even if your plea for help remains unanswered.

God is always good. His mercies are always new each morning. After the Light dawns, He continues to shine brighter and brighter.

Rejoice in Him today! Watch as His Light begins to shine brighter around you, just like the dawn.

Today's Prayer CHALLENGE:

REJOICE FOR TEN

Write down ten reasons to rejoice. Want a challenge? Choose ten reasons to rejoice in the midst of a dark circumstance.

Today's Prayer FOCUS:

EXTENDED TRIALS

Yesterday, we prayed through those situations that disrupt the lovely plans we expected for our homeschools. Each day holds a variety of minor disruptions.

Sometimes, the disruptions linger for an extended period of time. Extended trials of chronic illness, caregiving for a loved one, and drawn-out relational conflicts refuse to pause for regularly scheduled school time.

Over time, these extended trials create a darkness. The darkness of extended trials can threaten to drown you. Ask me how I know. I've looked up at the swirling waves and gasped for air more than once. During these times, rest is the last word to describe my heart.

Just as light shines best in darkness, so can rest in chaos. Keep seeking Jesus first. He passionately cares for you in the midst of whatever is going on. He has an amazing way of turning everything into good. Hang on in faith.

Rate the restfulness of your heart with extended trials:

1 2 3 4 5 6 7 8 9 10

1=Anxious/weary/striving 10=Calm/trusting/restful

EVALUATE

What extended trials are you trying to survive?

____

____

____

What words describe the state of your heart in the midst of these trials?

____

____

____

SURRENDER

How have you been trying to create a sense of rest for yourself? Will you surrender these efforts to Jesus?

____

____

____

Will you choose to trust and rejoice even if the circumstances never change?

____

____

____

RECEIVE

Write out a prayer asking God to give you grace and rest.

____

____

____

Ask God for *one thing* you can do to cultivate rest during your extended trials.

____

____

____

NOTES

____

____

____

____

____

____

____

____

continue

day twenty-one

MY HEART ALWAYS SANK AS WE DROVE THROUGH THE GATE. My family vacationed every year in the same condominium in South Carolina. Every year, as we drove out on Sunday morning, my heart felt heavy with disappointment over the end of our weeklong vacation.

The sinking feeling continues as an adult. Only now, the reality of daily adult life stares me in the face at the end of a vacation –laundry, cooking, cleaning, teaching. A brief break of rest is enjoyable, but daily life must resume. As much as I might long for vacation to continue, the end is really the end.

The end of 21 Days of focused prayer, however, is not the same! The end of this purposeful season is more of a beginning.

We celebrate a commencement ceremony at the end of an academic journey. In one sense, it's the end. But the word "commence" really means "to begin." This is the type of ending we encounter today; it's an ending that is truly a beginning.

Today is certainly not the end of a journey. For the past three weeks (or perhaps a bit longer), you have been building new habits. You have been laying a foundation of seeking Jesus first. You have been asking God for rest in the midst of real-life circumstances.

So our challenge today is simply to continue. Tomorrow is Day 22, but keep on going! Continue setting time aside each day to be in His Word and talk with Him through prayer. Continue trying something new to draw yourself closer to His heart. Continue seeking Him first for a restful homeschool.

Choose one new habit and continue. You could begin a habit of gratitude and thank God for at least ten things each morning. For a habit of joy, choose to rejoice daily for something related to your biggest struggle. Or turn up the music to build a habit of worship.

Read through your notes and consider the prayers you have prayed. How has God already answered? How are you learning to trust even if He's not answering yet? Will you believe He has more in store for you than you can even imagine?

> *"Now to Him who is able to do far more abundantly beyond all that we ask or think, according to the power that works within us, to Him be the glory in the church and in Christ Jesus to all generations forever and ever. Amen."*
> *Ephesians 3:20-21*

Far. More. Abundantly. Beyond.

Those requests and needs you've been praying about? God can do more. That name of God you've been asking Him to reveal? God can do more. The change you want in your heart? God can do more.

Don't stop now. You have begun an excellent habit. Don't stop when it's just getting good. Continue. Watch for God to do far more abundantly beyond all you can ask or imagine.

Today's Prayer CHALLENGE:

CHOOSE A NEW HABIT

Write out Ephesians 3:20:

___

___

___

What have been your favorite prayer challenges from the past 21 days?

___

___

___

Which ONE will you build into a habit? How?

___

___

___

How will you seek Jesus first tomorrow?

___

___

___

Today's Prayer FOCUS:

TODAY

Jesus cautioned against worrying about the future. Tomorrow will hold enough worries of its own. So let's focus on today. Rest is like manna, a gift to be enjoyed today.

As we close our journey, continue building a habit to carry you into Day 22 and beyond. Seek Jesus first each day for a restful heart so you can lead your family toward a restful homeschool. Evaluate how restful your heart is *today* and look for your current cues of unrest. Surrender your efforts to fix any problems without Jesus and release your expectations of the outcome. Ask God to reveal one step you can take to cultivate rest, and receive the rest only He can give.

Then repeat tomorrow.

Rate the restfulness of **your heart** in general:

1 2 3 4 5 6 7 8 9 10

1=Anxious/weary/striving 10=Calm/trusting/restful

Rate the restfulness of your **homeschool**:

1 2 3 4 5 6 7 8 9 10

1=Anxious/weary/striving 10=Calm/trusting/restful

EVALUATE

How is you heart more restful than on Day 1?

____

____

____

What are your current cues that you can still grow in rest and need to draw close to Jesus?

____

____

____

SURRENDER

Will you surrender your expectations of today to Jesus and trust Him with it?

____

____

____

Write out Psalm 90:17. Consider writing it in several versions.

____

____

____

Write out a prayer asking God to take your work today and establish His purpose in it.

____

____

____

____

RECEIVE

Write out a prayer asking God to give you grace and rest.

____

____

____

____

____

Ask God for *one thing* you can do to cultivate rest today.

____

____

____

____

____

____

NOTES

ABOUT THE AUTHOR

Aimee Smith and her husband, Aron, are second-generation homeschoolers who live just outside Birmingham, Alabama, with their four children, Jackson, Malyn, Micah, and Caleb. When not homeschooling, they enjoy camping, swimming, hiking, and biking together. On tired evenings after a long day, you could find them snuggled on the sofa watching *Wheel of Fortune* or *I Love Lucy.*

The past eleven years of their homeschool journey have held many surprises. One defining factor in their homeschool is their 10+ year battle with Aimee's autoimmune disease. Another has been their family's unexpected ministry as Aimee has been a local team leader with Classical Conversations since 2012. Over the years, they have learned God's plan for their homeschool is always better than their own.

As homeschool mom to four children, Aimee lives in the daily tension between God's call to the hard work of homeschooling and His call to rest as His daughter. As a homeschool community leader, her message to moms is to receive rest by clinging to Jesus and His promise of victory. Aimee is passionate about utilizing academics as a tool for discipleship, encouraging moms to seek rest in our busy days, and seeing our culture transformed through families committed to Jesus.

Join Aimee at aimeesmith.com for encouragement to cultivate a restful heart so you can experience victorious rest in your homeschool.

ADDITIONAL RESOURCES

Access additional resources for your 21-day journey with *The Restful Homeschool Resolution* on our private page:

www.aimeesmith.com/21days
Password: **SeekJesusFirst**

Download free printables for reminders to seek Jesus first.
Find an upcoming online book club.
Access links referenced in this book.

Made in the
USA
Columbia, SC

78375080R00121